PRISONER OF TWO WARS

Brothers Sherriff and John Probert were born in Griffith, New South Wales.

Sherriff worked for over thirty years in teacher education in New South Wales and South Australia. He has a Master of Letters from the University of New England and a Master of Education from the University of Massachusetts. He has written for a range of educational publications and journals. Sherriff retired from Flinders University in 1997 and lives in Blackwood, South Australia.

John undertook his schooling in Griffith, and completed a Bachelor of Economics at Sydney University. He joined Ford Australia on the Graduate Management Scheme in the early sixties and was General Marketing Manager prior to his retirement in 1991. He lives in Donvale, Victoria.

PRISONER
OF TWO WARS

An Australian Soldier's Story

Sherriff Probert and John Probert

Wakefield
Press

Wakefield Press
17 Rundle Street
Kent Town
South Australia 5071

First published 2001

Cover designed by Len Caridi
Book edited and produced by Michael Deves, Adelaide
Printed and bound by Hyde Park Press, Adelaide

National Library of Australia
Cataloguing-in-Publication entry

    Probert, Sherriff.
    Prisoner of two wars: an Australian soldier's story.

    Bibliography.
    Includes index.
    ISBN 1 86254 554 5.

    1. Probert, Jack. 2. Prisoners of war – Australia –
    Biography. 3. World War, 1914–1918 – Prisoners and prisons.
    4. World War, 1939–1945 – Prisoners and prisons.
    I. Probert, John, 1939–   . II. Title.

355.113092

For Justin, Michaeli, Christopher, Andrew and David,
who we hope will now know a little more of their grandfather, Jack.

A portrait photograph of Jack Probert taken after he had enlisted in the Royal Fying Corps.

Contents

Authors' Note

We knew very little of our father. When he enlisted in 1940 we were far too young to have any real memories of him. Only years later, after the chance discovery of a letter, were we driven to find out more of this man and his remarkable and harrowing experiences.

As the months have mounted in the preparation of this book, so have our debts. We wish to express our gratitude to Lynette Silver for her continuous support, suggestions and criticisms of our manuscript throughout its preparation. We are also greatly indebted to Michael Deves whose creative ideas coupled with his thoughtful editing have so greatly enhanced our final story.

We have enjoyed generous help from many other individuals and institutions, in particular, Ted Guiton and Douglas Heath from Rankins Springs; Win Perrin; Maxine Wain; Joelie Hancock; Wally Quinlivan, who gave ungrudgingly of his time in pursuing significant family records; Len Caridi for his cover design; Brendan O'Keefe for his research efforts at the Australian War Memorial Library and National Archives; Bendigo Historical Society; staff at the Public Records Offices in both Victoria and the UK; the Green Jackets Museum; and Richard Probert for his invaluable support in unearthing significant family records and resources in England.

For permission to reproduce photographs we thank the Australian War Museum (AWM), the La Trobe Collection of the State Library of Victoria (SLV) and the Griffith Genealogical and Historical Society. We especially acknowledge Ruth McGann for permission to use her father's sketches of the Sandakan camp, and Bill Young, a survivor of Sandakan whose drawings are so poignantly relevant to this story.

Importantly, we wish to acknowledge Merryn and Kaye who, over the past three years, have not only forgiven us our obsession but have also graciously supported our need to tell this story.

Finally, we wish to thank Rod Wells, who represents our only living contact with our father, and whose courage and fortitude enabled him to survive the cruelty of Sandakan. He has been our inspiration.

Sherriff Probert
John Probert

From Faint Footprints

In the First World War more than 4,000 Australians were captured and interned for varying lengths of time in enemy prisoner-of-war camps. In the Second World War this number increased nearly eight-fold to 30,000, of whom a little over 22,376 were incarcerated in Japanese camps. Of those in the latter, 8,031 perished. This is the singular story of Jack Probert, who was a prisoner in both wars.

Jack was our father. When we, his two sons, Sherriff and John, look back from the midpoint of our lives to what we remember and know about him, we realise how incomplete our understanding has been of a life that turned out to be so eventful and adventurous. Life for both of us has always been absorbing, and musings about his life and questions of his endowment to his family have simply sat quietly and unchallenged at the back of our minds for most of our lives.

What changed all that was a letter.

On the first day of September in 1973 our mother, who lived alone in the Riverina town of Griffith in south-west New South Wales, died unexpectedly. John, her youngest son, had just arrived back in Melbourne from a business trip to Detroit when the news arrived. Sherriff, his elder brother, had just left Australia to take up a one-year teaching appointment at an American university. Difficult as the circumstances were, it was decided after long telephone conver-sations that it would be best for John to manage the funeral arrange-ments, and take the lead in sorting out what needed to be done – what should be disposed of and what decisions could be kept for later resolution.

In the sad process of drawing to a close our mother's life, masses of papers and letters she had kept carefully for years were bundled into boxes and sent to John's home in Melbourne with the intention of dealing with them on Sherriff's return. As it turned out, these papers were to rest largely untouched in a garden shed in Melbourne for almost a quarter of a century.

In the course of looking through some of these papers a couple of years ago searching for some old photographs, a letter came to light that was both intriguing and challenging. It had been written by a soldier who, for just over twelve months between 1942 and 1943, had been incarcerated with Jack in Sandakan, North Borneo, one of the most notoriously brutal of the Japanese POW camps.

We had always known that Jack had been held in a POW camp. We knew that the circumstances had been almost unimaginable. But we had learned very little else. Minimal information had been passed to the family by the Australian military authorities. With a paternalism that typified the era, the authorities had decided that the circumstances surrounding the fate of these men were too horrific to know – in the interests of the families, the less said the better.

With its discovery over fifty years later this letter became the mainspring for us to find out not only more about Jack's time in Sandakan, but more importantly, his life.

Incomplete records – faint tracks

A significant part of the difficulty which lay tantalisingly in front of us was the incompleteness of the evidence relating to Jack. So little in the way of objects or stories appeared to remain. 'Footprints' of his track through life were in some places barely perceptible, in others simply non-existent. Photographs remaining in tattered, incomplete albums, laced with idiosyncratic and therefore enigmatic captions, conveyed little meaning or relevance across the years. There were scatterings of faded postcards and letters, but even these, without some ready framework of meaning, made little sense. The person who might have been able to answer many of the questions we were only now ready to ask – our mother, his wife – had been dead for many years.

What made it still more difficult was that we both retained few actual memories of Jack. We were far too young when he had left home for the last time. Try as he might, Sherriff's only memories were limited to three, when he was less than four years old. And we know how such early memories can become so easily distorted with the passage of time. At times it becomes almost impossible to decide if the recollections actually happened, or occurred in the way they have been remembered. More often than not they remain mere glimpses into the past that have little meaning or context. For instance, Sherriff thinks he can vaguely remember wandering out from where he was sleeping into a blazing light in a room at a time when we lived on a farm. He must have been no more than two years old. A loud, noisy and boisterous party was well in train and strange people stood around busily talking and drinking. There was a cacophony of noise, and people were spilling out of the house onto the hard, flattened, red dusty ground just outside the front door. He recalls his father spotting him standing bewildered at the bedroom door and sweeping him up without a word and returning him to the safety and darkness of his room. Blackout.

Another memory. Sherriff is a little older and in a different house, and apparently a little less in awe of this man who this time was wearing a woollen, khaki uniform. He suspects he must have said or done something that was less than acceptable. His father chased him with what he quickly realised was the clear intention of administering a suitable punishment. With the misplaced overconfidence of the young, and convinced that his superior leg speed would easily out-pace this man's, he still remembers the feeling of utter dismay and disbelief in rounding the corner of the verandah and finding the door locked and his retreat blocked. Punishment was duly delivered.

And then, through a heavy veil of memory, we both hold a similar, fleeting image of a figure rushing away from the house across vacant open ground chasing a train that had already left the station and was slowly gathering speed. We recall the extended arms of other men clad in khaki uniforms reaching down from the train's open door and Jack being swept up inside a carriage before turning to wave.

We now know that our father was on his way to join the Eighth Division of the Second AIF, due to leave within days for a confrontation with the Japanese forces on the Malayan peninsula.

Other faint prints had been left behind. Not unexpectedly, some we discovered while we were growing up. Others, and perhaps more significant ones, have only been exposed since. They left us stunned, not only by the serendipity and unexpectedness of their discovery, but also by the uniqueness of what they now represent. A track through life, step by surprising step, has gradually emerged to reveal a man who, in a short fifty-one years, not only confronted and challenged life with bravado and at times an extraordinary recklessness, but who was almost always prepared to chase what he hoped might be just beyond the next horizon.

A life of which we knew so little for decades has at last become visible.

CHAPTER 1

The Early Years

The reconstruction of Jack's story began simply with the letter. In mid 1996 in a search for missing photographs amongst our mother's personal papers John came across a number of old, faded letters held together with a rubber band. Shuffling through them quickly one of the letters caught his attention. Written on ordinary lined pad paper, it was dated 27 December 1945 and had a North Essendon address in the top right hand corner. As he scanned its contents the letter took on considerable significance.

The letter was a personal account of a friendship between the writer and our father whilst they were prisoners in the infamous Sandakan POW camp in North Borneo. It talked briefly of their initial meeting in the camp and what had drawn the two of them together. It spoke of the writer's brutal experiences with the Japanese, and the last time he had seen Jack. The signature at the end of the letter was 'Roderick G. Wells'.

It presented a conundrum. Here was a letter from someone who had survived Sandakan. And yet for years we had been led to believe that only six Australians had survived its brutality and horrors. We did not know of anyone by the name of Wells among them. Yet here was someone who had been a friend of Jack in Sandakan.

John then discovered a second letter from this man which explained a little more. It talked about how the two of them had helped each other when they were ill and told of conversations they shared during the long, hot evenings in Sandakan. Wells was taken away in July 1943 by the Japanese to Kuching for trial and likely execution for espionage activities, leaving Jack behind.

These two letters to our mother set us both wondering. We began to realise that the more we thought about our father the less we really knew about him, particularly his years in Sandakan. Rod Wells appeared to be the only man we now knew of who had actually known Jack in Sandakan. Yet by our calculations if Wells were still alive he would be close to ninety years old, and considering the deprivations of the Sandakan experience we both thought it unlikely that he would have achieved such an advanced age. But we were very intrigued. We decided to trace this man.

The first step was to telephone the Returned Servicemen's League in Melbourne. Advising them that at best he was riding a long shot, John asked if they could help him to trace the family of a Lieutenant Rod Wells. Within minutes the answer came: 'Yes, actually we have a Colonel R.G. Wells who is a member of the RSL in Rushworth.'

It was as simple as that. But for hours John delayed the call. What should he say? Was this expecting too much after more than fifty years? What if Wells had put all of this behind him and found such a call intrusive?

A man's voice answered. 'Is that Lieutenant Roderick Wells who once was a Japanese POW in Sandakan?'

'Yes,' came the reply.

'I am John Probert, son of John Probert, a Sandakan POW. Did you perhaps know him?'

What followed was one of those seemingly interminable silences, but intuitively John knew that the lengthy silence to his second question was a poignant 'Yes'. Even though he had steeled himself beforehand for this situation he found himself unnerved. He knew we had found someone who might be able to give us a first-hand account of Jack's experience in Sandakan.

This was an emotionally charged beginning to a lasting friendship between Rod and us, limited since only by Rod's advancing years and increasing frailty. Rod put us in contact with Lynette Silver (official historian for the Eighth Division) whose friendship and acclaimed book, *Sandakan: A Conspiracy of Silence,* not only helped put the horrors of Sandakan into a context for us, but more importantly started us on this personal odyssey of discovery.

With Rod Wells's and Lynette Silver's painstaking help, we pieced together some of our father's experiences in World War 2. But as each new piece of information came to us, the conundrums solved were matched by new ones generated. Our efforts were further complicated by the fact that Jack had used several names; variants of his real name, and even aliases.

We learned that Jack had enlisted in 1941 and gone to Singapore, but we also learned that he had enlisted once before this (in 1940), been sent overseas and then mysteriously discharged before 'successfully' enlisting a second time. Then, as we began to uncover details of his early life, we found some mysterious 'skeletons' in the family closet. As we followed his and his own father's family life, we found that both were married a second time after an unhappy first marriage. Intriguing parallels with the past marked Jack's life.

Jack's early life

Of all of the phases of Jack's life those of his early years were by far the most difficult to construct. The reconstruction began with a careful reading of a letter written by Jack as a sixteen-year-old from the sailing ship *Marian Woodside*, where, almost in passing, he expressed regret for difficulties he had caused his stepmother prior to leaving home. It struck us that not only did we know little of this stepmother, we knew *nothing* of his actual mother, apart from a name on Jack's birth certificate. Working on an assumption that his mother might have died early in the marriage, we diligently searched the Victorian records for a death certificate within what we considered a reasonable period. Failing to locate any record of her death, we decided the other possibility was to search the state's divorce records. An enquiry to the Supreme Court of Victoria confirmed that Maud Mary and Charles Probert had been divorced in 1901. At last we seemed to be getting somewhere. However, this all came to a grinding halt when we applied to the Prothonotary of the Supreme Court to view the divorce affidavits and our request was flatly denied. We argued that the divorce was now almost 100 years old; both parties to the petition were now deceased and the protagonists were our grandparents. But to no avail. We had struck a dead end.

Then came one of those serendipitous leads. A friend suggested to John that a search of the divorce records held in the Public Records Office in Laverton might be a useful alternative. And a few weeks later, there, incredibly, in an old hand-written court record book, we discovered what turned out to be the thread that unravelled this first part of the story. Of the 149 divorces filed in 1901 in Victoria there were two files on Probert vs Probert, one dated March, the other August. A search revealed that the March file was missing. That turned out to be the petition, Maud Mary Probert vs Charles Probert, submitted in March 1901 by Maud Mary, and clearly the one the Supreme Court had sourced from the Public Records Office to answer John's enquiry. But then came the surprise. John was casually informed that the second file, Charles Probert vs Maud Mary submitted in August 1901 by Charles, was still held in the archives and available simply on request.

John could not believe his luck. Within fifteen minutes of requesting the file he held in his hand the petition for divorce written in a fine copperplate hand; it revealed the stark history of a disruptive and turbulent marriage. We had discovered a critical, if perhaps coloured, source of information about Jack's first five years of life.*

While this was an invaluable beginning we now needed to know about Jack's family background and origins. Like our experience with his parents' divorce this too was a journey of discovery. The lead came this time from the death certificate of Jack's father. Amongst details on the certificate we found the names of his father's parents, who we deduced from other information that we already possessed might have come to Victoria as free settlers sometime in the mid 1850s. We set out to trace their arrival in Australia.

We pored over hundreds of ships' arrival records in the Public Records Office, covering almost a forty-year period in the middle of the nineteenth century, eagerly but unsuccessfully seeking some clue to their arrival. It was on a return visit days later to double-check the files that John discovered what he was looking for. From the screen of the microfiche machine leapt the names of Jack's grandparents on

---

* We subsequently obtained Maud Mary's petition, which provided further insights into the turbulent marriage.

In the Supreme Court of the ~~State~~ ~~Colony~~ of Victoria } Divorce and Matrimonial Causes Jurisdiction

1901 No.

Between Charles Moule Verdon Probert   Petitioner

and

Maud Mary Probert   Respondent

I Charles Moule Verdon Probert of 130 Rathmines Road Auburn in the State of Victoria Insurance Broker make oath and say as follows:-

1. I am the Petitioner herein

2. I was lawfully married to the abovenamed Respondent on the 7th day of August 1889 at St Marks Church Golden Square Bendigo in the said State by the Reverend Robert Buchanan a minister of the Church of England and according to the rites of that Church

3. I am now of the age of 42 years and was born at Williamstown in the said State on the 30th day of March 1859 as I am informed and verily believe and the Respondent is now of the age of 29 years and was born in Bendigo aforesaid on or about the 23rd day of October 1871 as I am informed and verily believe

4. That I and the Respondent are now and for upwards of two years have been domiciled in the said State

5. That prior to my marriage with Respondent I lived at View Street Bendigo aforesaid and was then out of employment, but had previously been a Bank Manager and the Respondent lived with her Mother at Bendigo aforesaid and was a Spinster Subsequent to my marriage I was a Stock and Share Broker then a Clerk and later on an Insurance Broker, which business I still carry on and my wife when living apart from me lived on the income which she derived from her father's estate.

The initial page of the petition for divorce:
Charles Probert vs Maud Mary, submitted in August 1901.

Jack's grandfather, William Richard
Probert 1815–1903

Jack's father, Charles Moule Verdon
Probert 1855–1917

Elsie May Probert, Jack's stepmother,
1888–1939

Jack Probert, aged about 2

the handwritten manifesto of a ship called the *Protector,* which had arrived in Melbourne Port in May 1853. This proved invaluable. Not only did it turn out that the husband, Captain William Probert, was the common ancestor of the current English and Australian branches of the family, but from this discovery we were able to pursue this English connection to their family home of Bevils on the outskirts of the small village of Bures in Suffolk. The search that followed unlocked a wealth of information, including correspondence written by William during the 1830s and 1840s, and journals and writings about him by his sister much later in the nineteenth century. At the same time we discovered a further collection of fascinating correspondence between Jack's father and his half-brother, written in the years between 1876 and 1885. While many of the letters from this exchange simply conveyed the usual family news, some written by Jack's father in particular contained long and fascinating descriptions of his life and adventures in the harsh outback of Australia during the 1880s.

These sets of correspondence of Jack's father and grandfather helped us begin assembling a more detailed and personal picture of Jack's immediate family. (Appendix 3 provides a brief time-line.) More importantly they began to gradually reveal to us for the first time something of the origins of Jack's spirit and adventurousness, demonstrated so amply later in his own life. In order to make these connections it is necessary to take a short detour back to the Australia of the goldrush years.

Jack's grandfather, William Probert

William Richard Probert was an extraordinary man who turned his hand to a number of vocations throughout his long and spirited life. At different times he had been an adventurer, a sea captain, a gold prospector, a ship's surveyor, a commission agent and lay preacher, and all-in-all appears to have been a strong and resolute father-figure.

William left school in Essex, England in 1832 at the age of seventeen, became a midshipman in the Royal British Navy and made a number of voyages to the West Indies, along the east coast of the American colonies and as far north as Newfoundland and Nova Scotia.

In 1835 William joined the East India Company as a midshipman, sailing first on the *Recovery* then the *Adrian*. He spent four years visiting far-flung and exotic ports from Canton to Calcutta, trading for the Company throughout the Far East in spices, tea and silk. He even spent time in Hobart in the latter part of 1835, at a time when the more hard-bitten and recalcitrant convicts transported to the colonies were being sent to hell-holes like Port Arthur and Sarah Island.

In 1842 William gained his First Class Certificate and became a First Officer on the *Captain Nelson*. When he gained his Master's Certificate in 1845 he captained the *Isabella* and the *City of Puna* on a number of voyages to India and the Far East for the East India Company. He relates in letters to his family many of his experiences on these voyages: a mutiny in Hobart, a rescue of stranded sailors off Booby Island, sailing though the treacherous shoals of the Torres Straits in Northern Australia, being attacked by the Dutch in the East Indies, purchasing rice from the Queen of Lombok and trading with the Chinese. They read like stories straight from the pages of a *Boys' Own Annual*.

In 1850, aged 35, William met and married Elizabeth Archer, the youngest of three daughters of a family from Saffron Walden in Essex. However, in the early years of their marriage the couple tragically lost three stillborn sons in succession. The loss of their third child might have significantly influenced them in their decision to migrate to the Victorian colony to start a new life. The discovery of gold in the colony must have also been a powerful magnet. When the news first reached England it was mostly young and single men who rushed off in a spirit of adventure to make their fortunes and return home as quickly as possible. But by the time William and Elizabeth made their decision, the character of migration was becoming more purposeful and calculated. Married couples and families were beginning to migrate permanently to the colonies. People were recognising the growing prosperity of the colony, which offered business and professional opportunities, and high wages. At the least, the couple thought they should give Victoria a serious trial for a few years. It was in this context that in May 1853 William and Elizabeth, along with

Melbourne's port around the time of William and Elizabeth's arrival.
'Sandridge from Hobson's Bay', lithograph by Francois Cogne, 1863.

129 other passengers, left England for Melbourne in the sailing ship
Protector.

When they arrived in Port Phillip Bay in August 1853 after three
long months Melbourne's harbour was filled with a vast assortment
of London and Liverpool ships, each disgorging small boats filled to
the gunwales with people and possessions. Alongside them were
vessels from ports all over the world, bringing to Victoria thousands
of gold miners seeking their fortunes.

Newly arrived ships generally anchored well out in the bay, and
flotillas of lighters carried passengers to a beach that provided easiest
access to the city. At the time the spot (in the present Port Melbourne
area) was known as 'The Beach'. Covered by tea-tree scrub, it was
graced with only two buildings, both conveniently public houses.
Most passengers faced a long walk from the beach to a point in the
river just above 'The Falls'. After a dusty trudge of about two
kilometres travellers crossed the river in a punt or ferry boat before
continuing their walk to the outskirts of the city at a point roughly in
line with the site of the Western Market of the early 1900s.

William and Elizabeth were fortunate enough to be able to afford a river steamer which took them from the *Protector* along the Yarra to one of four busy wharves close to Flinders Street, at the western end of the city.

At that time Melbourne was undergoing a rapid transformation, changing from a pastoral and rural settlement and acquiring the feel and institutions of an embryonic city. Its recently acquired independence from NSW in 1850 and the extraordinary gold strikes in the following year had provided impetus for these changes. Nevertheless the countryside lay just beyond Lonsdale Street, and all around the burgeoning city were market gardens and orchards, paddocks of wheat and oats, and small dairy farms.

This transformation and the increase in numbers brought severe difficulties. The avalanche of migrants exerted enormous pressures on the emerging city. Two years before the Proberts arrived in the colony the city's population had hovered around 20,000. By the year of their arrival in 1853 it had exploded to 140,000. The city's services were stretched to their limits, and in some cases unable to cope.

One particularly serious problem was housing and accommodation. On disembarking William and Elizabeth found that almost every available space in hotels and lodging houses had already been occupied. Those who had tents pitched them. Others constructed primitive gunyahs along the river, in the eastern and western market reserves, or in the scrub between the beach and the city. Many were forced to spend their first night, or longer, on the wharves among barrels and bales, making shelters from planks, baggage and blankets.

The worst problem was what to do with luggage. Many settlers had brought all their household chattels, only to find that they could not afford to have much of it landed, as storage space was severely limited and expensive. The mattresses and bedding, for example, that newly arrived passengers threw overboard littered beaches for years to come. Others began to sell what they could. Sitting near the wharf they pathetically offered for sale watches, clothes, guns, pistols, books and furniture that they had brought with them. In fact the gathering in front of the Customs House became known as the 'Rag Fair'. Later, when regular traders began to move in, it developed into a popular market place for Melbourne's citizenry.

Collins Street, Melbourne, looking west along Elizabeth Street, in the 1850s.

SLV 817065

'Tent city'. Canvas Town, between Princess Bridge and South Melbourne in the 1850s.

Most stayed as briefly as possible in Melbourne before leaving for the diggings. William and Elizabeth almost immediately took to the road for the gold diggings in Bendigo (at the time called Sandhurst) a few hundred kilometres north-west of Melbourne. Gold had been discovered there just a little over a year previously, and the strike, claimed to be one of the world's richest alluvial deposits ever found, quickly attracted thousands of diggers.

At William and Elizabeth's first view of the 'diggings' in August of that year they would have been confronted with a labyrinth of canvas, calico and bark, and a seething, restless population of close to 23,000 diggers. They would have seen holes like gravel pits everywhere, and heard the steady din of hundreds of rocking cradles. The grass had disappeared, the trees had been laid waste, and everywhere was mud, slush, puddles and shovelled piles of yellow soil.

SLV 1116033

Bendigo in the 1850s.
'Bendigo, from the Road to Eagle Hawk', lithograph by J. Tingle, 1857.

Normally, most newcomers would settle on a claim, take out their licences and next day begin digging their holes. Interestingly, William and Elizabeth set about establishing a small chandlery store, selling basic groceries and a variety of mining essentials such as candles, oil, soap, paint, cordage and canvas. William, it seems, had quickly realised that a shopkeeper could equally make his fortune, without relying to the same extent as the digger on the vagaries of 'lady luck'. There is little doubt, nevertheless, that William in his time on the diggings devoted a great deal of time to prospecting.

The Bendigo chandlery flourished for William and Elizabeth and it seemed that their gamble to migrate to Victoria had been well vindicated. However, early in their second year in Bendigo tragedy struck. In March 1855 Elizabeth delivered her first child, Charles, but six weeks later she suddenly contracted typhus fever and died within days. Her death was a cruel twist. In a situation not unlike the one Charles would face some forty years further on, William was left a single, middle-aged father with a new-born son to raise.

William took the responsibility very seriously. In his time on the goldfields the chandlery business had continued to flourish, and he had also experienced more than passing good fortune as a prospector. Now, however, with an infant to care for, he decided it best to return to Melbourne where he anticipated that life would be more stable, and help with the care of an infant a little easier to come by. Within weeks of his wife's tragic death, William left Bendigo and moved to Melbourne. He rented premises in Flinders Lane on the outskirts of the city near the harbour, and set about establishing a new business, one for which it would appear he had strong credentials – a ship's surveying and commissioning service for the busy commercial ports of Melbourne and nearby Williamstown.

William spent seven years in this business, but in 1862, influenced by a growing desire to take Charles home to his family and at the same time attend to his son's education, he returned to England. He may also have wished to seek a new wife. The nature of migration to Victoria in the 1850s resulted in males outnumbering females by a ratio of over three-to-one. Within two years of returning, and just months shy of turning fifty, William met and married a widow, Lucinda Hunt, and in the following seven years raised a family of five half-brothers and one half-sister to the young Charles.

In 1872 Charles's father and step-mother separated. William and Charles, now aged 17, with his half-brothers, Will aged 8 and Arthur 7, returned to live in Australia. During their marriage William and Lucinda had become devout members of the Plymouth Brethren, and William a lay preacher. The Brethren were a strict Puritan sect of evangelical Christians who had broken away from the Anglican Church in Ireland in the late 1820s, crossed to England and established their first centre in Plymouth. An educated guess suggests that William had become deeply involved in the work of the Brethren in England and his separation gave him an opportunity to heed the call to 'carry the message to new fields'. The 'fields' he chose were those he already knew well, Melbourne. William devoted 17 years to being a Brethren preacher in and around Melbourne.

In 1889, at the age of 74, and becoming increasingly frail, William Richard Probert returned to England for the last time. At the age of

Bevils, the Probert family home, on the outskirts of the village of Bures, Suffolk.

87, this spirited adventurer died at the old Probert home of Bevils in Suffolk in 1903.

Jack's father

Young Charles arrived back in Melbourne with his father in 1872. He had spent ten years living in England and had just turned 17. As a result of the separation from his wife and the assumption of his new role as a preacher for the Brethren in Melbourne, William seems to have divested sizeable sums of money to various members of the family, including Charles. Unfortunately, it appears that within a relatively short period of time Charles, through what he describes as 'loose living and speculative endeavours', not only rapidly lost his 'inheritance' but managed to rack up additional substantial debts. These circumstances forced him to leave Melbourne for Albury with his 'swag and tin billy'. For the next few years he led a nomadic and precarious life looking for ways to repay his debts. His son, Jack, was to repeat this pattern some years later.

There is little doubt that the years of harsh and rough living that followed were instrumental in shaping and tempering the strong, hard-working but solitary disposition of Charles. He seems to have grown 'bush-smart' and adept at turning his hand to almost any job. He also gradually acquired a mature eye for good financial propositions, which later in life led him to become a successful stock-broker and a respected member of the Melbourne business and commercial fraternity.

After leaving Melbourne Charles moved about the country in New South Wales, Queensland and the Northern Territory, taking on droving and station-hand jobs to make money to pay off his debts. For most of this time, as he wrote in one of his letters, he lived on the 'smell of an oily rag'. This was the period of the early pioneering days of the cattle and sheep industry in eastern and central Australia, and pastoralists sought young, single, hardworking men to move cattle and sheep around the country for sale or agistment. There was plenty of work for those willing. In his letters of the late 1870s and early 1880s Charles mentions travelling through northern Victoria, the outback of NSW and into northern Queensland and the Northern Territory, droving large mobs of cattle and sheep over long distances and working as a station-hand on a number of properties.

Charles returned to Victoria from northern Australia in the middle of 1885, and some time later, and just prior to his marriage to Maud Mary, was employed as a bank clerk in Bendigo, the town in which his father and mother had briefly settled on their arrival in the colony thirty years previously.

Disruptions and upheavals

Jack was born in November 1893 at home in Curral Road in the leafy suburb of Elsternwick close to Melbourne's Port Philip Bay. His parents, Charles and Maud Mary, had been married for nearly four years but had suffered wretched marital difficulties from the outset of their marriage in Bendigo in 1889. From the beginning things simply went awry. Following the wedding ceremony Maud Mary, the youngest daughter of a large family of twelve, had quite extraordinarily returned straight from the church to her family home, and Charles, her rebuffed husband, was reluctantly forced to return by himself to his 'bachelor digs' in View Street just a block away from his new wife's family home. It took almost three years before Mary was willing to join Charles and finally consummate the marriage. What led to this strange happening is difficult to fathom. Why did she marry if she intended to remain with her mother? Was it simply a case of 'cold feet'? Was it related to the substantial age gap? The thirteen-year difference between them indicated on the marriage certificate may have in fact been greater, because Charles, in other circumstances, had demonstrated a readiness to massage his age whenever it seemed necessary or desirable. Also, the fact that it was a shared wedding ceremony (with Maud Mary's older sister) suggests a young girl too easily influenced by family expectations to marry, but realising its folly just a little too late and using the excuse of an ailing mother to avoid its consequences. Whatever the reasons, from this distance we can only wonder.

Nevertheless, in the ensuing three years Charles showed remarkable perseverance, constantly imploring his young wife to leave Bendigo and join him. During this time he moved from job to job, spending time in Tasmania employed in the mining business, followed by stints in the NSW Public Service, then with a wool company in Sydney. In October 1892 his persistence paid off. Following the death of her mother, Maud Mary finally decided to leave Bendigo and join Charles in Sydney. As employment prospects and accommodation in Sydney were less than satisfactory the couple decided to move to Melbourne. They rented a home in Elsternwick and a year later Jack was born.

There is little doubt that, from the outset, marriage and motherhood sat uneasily with Maud Mary. In May 1894, after months of continual arguments and without her husband's knowledge, Maud Mary unexpectedly disposed of all the household furniture and with her six-month-old son left Melbourne and returned to Bendigo. Despite repeated and desperate requests from Charles she refused to return, and through her solicitor informed her husband she was no longer prepared to live with him. (Maud Mary had independent means.) Moreover, she told him, she had decided to return their son to him accompanied by a charge nurse. On 28 June Jack was duly delivered to his father's office.

Surprisingly, within a couple of months the two managed to patch up their differences. In September 1894 they recommenced their stormy marriage, this time in a new home in the bayside suburb of

Charles Probert at Elsternwick, with a young Jack.

St Kilda. But the relationship barely survived another two years before Maud Mary, in virtually a repeat performance, sold the furniture and again departed with Jack, now almost two-and-half-years old. Charles was left with a note from her solicitor informing him that this time she intended to be free of the marriage and planned to petition for divorce as soon as possible.

In the early weeks of this final separation, Charles managed to see his son a number of times through a proctorial arrangement, but in March 1898, in a continuation of her strange, impulsive behaviour, Maud Mary boarded the SS *Cintra* with Jack and sailed from Melbourne to Sydney, where she remained until January 1900. Then, unexpectedly and without explanation, Jack, now aged six, was returned to live permanently with his father in Melbourne. Charles was 45.

It is intriguing how patterns in life can sometimes be repeated between generations. Charles himself had experienced a similar difficult and uncertain start to life, losing his mother at birth and being brought up by a single, middle-aged father who, whenever life went awry, remained a caring, strong support.

Early in 1901 divorce petitions were finally lodged by both Maud Mary and Charles, and by the end of the year Jack's parents were divorced.

Growing up in Melbourne

As has been outlined, Jack's first five years of life were turbulent and disruptive as he found himself passed between his warring parents. It was only when Charles finally obtained custody that his son's life returned to any degree of normality.

Charles's business opportunities had begun to flourish and by the time the divorce was finalised in 1901 he seems to have at last found a solid and promising business vocation in stock and insurance broking. As his fortunes improved, he established himself in Stalbridge Chambers in Little Collins Street in the financial centre of Melbourne. Homes he bought in Malvern and Kooyong reflected his rising business affluence, as did invitations to important Melbourne events such as the celebration of the opening of Parliament by the Duke and Duchess of Cornwall and York in the Exhibition Building in May 1901.

As a result of this increasing affluence, Charles was able to enrol Jack in 1905 in Cumloden School in Alma Road, east St Kilda, which was a private preparatory school for the prestigious Melbourne Grammar.

In July of the same year, Charles, now 50, and having been a bachelor for a number of years, rather unexpectedly married a 20-year-old Dutch girl, Elsie May Vanden Hooten, in a Methodist ceremony in East Brighton. In the following February, Elsie May gave birth to a half-brother for Jack.

Despite an eventful year from the unexpected marriage, moving into a new home in Inverness Street in Malvern and new family circumstances, Jack performed well in his studies and completed his preparatory year at Cumloden with excellent results in Algebra, Divinity, Latin, French, Geography, English and Arithmetic, although he was slightly less successful in History and Euclid.

Church of England Grammar School, Melbourne, in 1905. Jack was enrolled there in February 1906, at the age of twelve.

The young schoolboy: Jack in his Melbourne Grammar uniform.

In 1906 Jack was enrolled as a twelve-year-old at Melbourne Grammar. Records of this time are sparse and incomplete, so we are not sure how long he spent at the school. Nevertheless, Melbourne Grammar appears, as we have since discovered, to have left an indelible impression on Jack. There is mention in the *Melburnian*, the school's magazine, of his entry as a new boy along with 85 others into the Senior School in February of that year, and a record of him passing his swimming test in March. Not surprisingly, the school emphasised patriotism and service to King and country, and Old Melburnians' military service records were celebrated and lauded in special service books, the school magazine, school prayers, songs, plaques and stained glass windows in the school's chapel. Descriptions of Jack's wartime exploits were published in the school's magazine in 1920 and 1946. (These were not always accurate, as we subsequently discovered!)

However when Jack left school things started to go off the rails. His father's health became a cause for concern, and with it came worries with the business. There were also signs of difficulty for Elsie May – her husband was almost 30 years her senior, with established work habits and lifestyle. In fact, Jack was only a few years younger than Elsie May, and his youthful outlook was probably far closer to his step-mother's than was hers to her husband.

Rebelliousness not atypical of adolescence, age gaps rather greater than the usual, and Jack's strong streak of independence led progressively to family friction. There is evidence that Jack might well have been sent to stay for extended periods with relatives and friends who lived close by. Whatever the case, in 1910, after continuing rows and upsets, Jack finally collected his belongings and, aged sixteen, left home.

CHAPTER 2

Skeletons in the Cupboard

After he left his Melbourne home Jack's unruly behaviour created serious concerns for his family. Impetuous and youthful indiscretions led him into conflict with the law, and he found himself forced to live by his wits, looking for work and lodgings. It would be almost two years before he realised the aimlessness of what he was doing and the need to make a significant change to his life.

Reconstructing the time between Jack leaving school and the beginning of the First World War proved a challenge. There were no stories from the usually reliable family grapevine, and the only relevant material that we had from the period were the small number of letters written by Jack from on board the sailing ship *Marian Woodside* in 1910. For a long time we surmised that Jack had left school and in the period prior to the outbreak of the First World War spent his time sailing the world. We endeavoured to trace the route of the *Marian Woodside* through various records, such as the Registers of Ships' Crews, and in a range of places, from the National Maritime Museum of Greenwich to the Maritime Archives in Newfoundland. Our search proved fruitless.

This led us back to the only evidence we held, the letters, and in particular the two written by Jack to his father from the *Marian Woodside* in Sydney Port in August 1910. In these letters, two separate comments began to take on new meaning. First:

> Dad, I am grateful to you and Mr Fraser and all the others that helped me out of such an awful place. I signed on at three o'clock this afternoon as boy …

And second:

> My mother has not a scrap of affection for me now. She wouldn't
> even come to see me at Darlinghurst ...

These two comments became the vital keys that began to unlock
the mystery.

At various time we had both lived in Sydney. After leaving school
John had attended Sydney University, and in the early 1960s Sherriff
had taught for a time at Seaforth on the North Shore. On tram rides
from the city to the eastern suburbs we had often passed the old
Sydney Law Courts in Darlinghurst. Suddenly the penny dropped.
'Darlinghurst' meant law courts, and Jack's comments 'out of that
awful place' and 'my mother wouldn't visit me' took on a darker
meaning: trouble with the law. Our suspicions were more or less
confirmed when we discovered that at the turn of the century
Darlinghurst had been the principal gaol of New South Wales.

We had found the critical thread. With Lynette Silver's help we set
about looking for court records in the NSW State Archives that
might have involved Jack. We discovered that in May 1911 Jack had
been sentenced to hard labour and incarcerated for six months in the
Darlinghurst gaol. In addition, the court and prison records revealed
that not only had he been using aliases in this period, he also had a
Victorian police record.

We returned to Victoria to examine the Victorian *Police Gazette*s
in the Public Library of Victoria, in which, amongst a variety of other
matters, State court proceedings were regularly reported. In the July
1910 edition of the *Police Gazette*, John discovered a listing of Jack's
appearance in May of that year at a Petty Sessions hearing in the
Victorian country town of Castlemaine. Unfortunately details of the
courts' proceedings were not included in the *Gazette*s. To obtain this
information John visited the Public Records Office in Laverton
where in one of the large leather-bound journals, in the neat copperplate script of a court attendant, he discovered the lead he needed.
A visit to the State Library's newspaper records finally uncovered
what we had been seeking for so long, the details of Jack's first brush
with the law, colourfully written up in the daily editions of the two

local papers, the *Castlemaine Leader* and the *Mount Alexander Mail*.

We were now in a position to make sense of this next period of Jack's life.

Early indiscretions

When he first left home in early May 1910 Jack made his way to the Bendigo and Castlemaine district in the mid-north of Victoria to look for work, and at the same time try to meet up with members of his mother's family and their friends who, he knew, still lived in the Bendigo district. He reasoned that they might help him with useful contacts for work and accommodation.

However, in what turned out to be the first of a number of minor indiscretions, he fell foul of the law. Within a month he found himself for the first time spending a few lonely and uncomfortable nights in the local gaol.

His misdemeanour – in the time-honoured tradition of youth – appears to have been reckless and foolish. It had all the marks of a young man who simply wanted to impress a young woman. His idea must, at the time, have seemed an easy way to demonstrate his worldliness. He impetuously offered to take a young lady's photograph, without the means of fulfilling his rash promise. His solution was to visit one of the local stores and claim he wanted to buy a camera, on the promise that he would return and pay for it as soon as he had gained approval from his mother. In the meantime he would take the photograph, return the camera and no one would be any the wiser. The proprietor agreed to the arrangement, and perhaps with the prospect of additional purchases allowed Jack to take with him some extra items for the camera. In the surge of enthusiasm for his idea Jack probably had every intention of returning the camera as soon as he had impressed the girl. However, somewhere between the intention and the action – perhaps he was distracted for the rest of the day by his newly acquired girlfriend – he failed to return the goods to the store before it closed. The proprietor, thinking he had been duped, made his way to the local police station, and a young constable was quickly dispatched to the hotel where Jack was staying.

When confronted by the policeman's charge of larceny Jack, in a show of reckless adolescent bluster, first tried to persuade the policemen that he actually owned the camera. The claim fell on deaf ears; Jack was promptly arrested and, although by then admitting the foolishness of his prank, was escorted to the local gaol where he spent the next three nights in its cold and bleak stone cell behind the station.

At the hearing on the following Tuesday morning, Jack's legal representative argued strongly that Jack had had every intention of returning the camera but had foolishly delayed its return, and made matters worse with his ill-conceived act of bluff with the constable. From a distance his defence seems less than convincing, but the representations made by his legal representative and friends moved the magistrate towards leniency. Jack still received a sharp dressing down from the bench for his foolishness, and was fined a total of 40 shillings for what was then recorded as his first official misdemeanour.

In true local tradition, the following Friday's edition of the daily paper, the *Castlemaine Leader*, carried for the district's consumption the embarrassing details of Jack's public appearance in the town's Court of Petty Sessions.

In normal circumstances one might have expected Jack to return to Melbourne and patch up the dissension with his father. But it was not to be. Instead, attracted by the bright lights of Sydney, Jack insisted that he intended to make his own way in life. Within a couple of days of his court appearance he caught the train north.

Unfortunately for Jack this very action worsened his situation. By entering New South Wales Jack breached what was at the time known as the 'Influx of Criminals Prevention Act', which operated between the various states of Australia. The Act served to prevent individuals with police records leaving the state in which they had been convicted for a period of time stated by the courts. It is unclear whether Jack was unaware of this restriction or it was simply another act of bravado by a headstrong young man. Within three weeks of arriving in Sydney Jack found himself being questioned by police and locked in Darlinghurst Gaol. A week later, he appeared before a magistrate and was found guilty of breaching the Act; on 19 July he was sentenced, rather harshly, to six months imprisonment. The fact that he had foolishly given the police an alias probably did little to help his cause!

CASTLEMAINE POLICE COURT

This day before Messrs Odgers, Balwin and Newham, Js P [Justices of the Peace]

IMPOSITION

John William Probert pleaded guilty to a charge of imposing on Max Pincus for the value of a camera, the price of which was 10s 6d.

Mr Thwaites appeared on behalf of the accused.

Max Pincus stated that the camera produced was his property; it was obtained from him by the accused.

To Mr Thwaites – the camera was in as good a condition now as when supplied to the accused.

Thomas Graham Mitchell said on the 21st inst., accused came to Mr Pincus' shop and asked to see a Kodak camera. Accused said he would like to take the camera home to show his mother; permitted him to take the camera away, but it was not returned; accused came back and said the article would suit; he also ordered some other things, but did not return for them; did not know Probert but had seen him about the town.

Constable Crisfield deposed to arresting the accused; he had said he had purchased the camera in Melbourne; found this to be untrue, and then Probert said he had got the camera to take a young lady's photo. He had also said he had done a shabby trick, and was very sorry for it. Believed the accused intended to return the camera on Monday as stated.

Mr Thwaites said it was a case in which justice should be tempered with mercy. Probert was over the age for reformatory treatment. The facts did not disclose anything serious. The lad made a boyish boast to take a girl's photo, and he did so. He had no intention of retaining the camera, and when taxed with his conduct he confessed to having done a shabby trick. He had really gained no advantage nor tried to get any. Mr Thwaites asked the bench to allow the accused to be liberated on his own surety to come up for sentence when called on, or to impose a fine. He thought a fine would be preferable as perhaps a surety could not be found. If he were sent to gaol the chances were he might become a criminal.

He had been pretty well punished now by having been under arrest since Saturday last. Accused fully realised his position, and was desirous of leading a different life. Mr Thwaites asked for the best consideration the bench could give.

The bench said the charge was not a serious one, but the accused's position as a young man was a serious one. A good birching would do him good, and had it not been for his friends he would be sent to gaol. The bench had no desire to send accused to gaol but wished him to enter a useful life, and advised him to go to work, and cease flashing about the country.

A fine of £2 was imposed, in default distress.

The Castlemaine Leader, *Friday, 27 May 1910*

Jack's actions following this sentencing reflect the feelings of guilt he must now have experienced. It took him nearly two weeks before he could summon enough courage to contact his father for help. His father's quick representations, helped by a couple of well-connected friends in Sydney, proved sufficiently effective. Early on the morning of 17 August, after four weeks of Sydney's bleak and infamous Darlinghurst Gaol, Jack's sentence was revoked and he found himself unexpectedly released and placed 'on special remission'. In a matter of hours he had been taken by one of his father's friends to Neutral Bay, and by the middle of that afternoon he had signed on as a crew member of the British steel-sided windjammer, the *Marian Woodside*. (The *Marian Woodside* was the sister ship of the *Polly Woodside*, which today lies on public show in the Port of Melbourne.)

It would be reasonable to assume that a condition of his discharge agreement was that Jack demonstrate that he could put behind him the events of the previous few months and make a fresh start. Interestingly, his Darlinghurst experience had not dulled his wish for independence. He still wanted to make his own way, and the prospects of sailing the world in a windjammer were just too good to pass up. The decision to join the *Marian Woodside*, ready within the week to sail for Chile, was seemingly just such a demonstration of his wish to make a new start while remaining independent.

Jack's letter of apology and his explanation of the act of 'signing on' to his father on 17 August 1910, the very day he boarded the *Marian Woodside*, conveys some idea of the measure of relief he must have felt at his release from what he describes with considerable feeling as 'such an awful place'. It also shows the extent to which he appreciated how much his new employment was an opportunity for him to begin to redeem himself in the eyes of his family and friends:

> Dad I am grateful to you and Mr Fraser and all the others that helped me out of such an awful place … I signed on at 3 o'clock this afternoon as boy. My captain is James Fotheringham and all my shipmates are young men between 18 and 26 years of age and all Britishers. There are 3 mates and the crew is 26 all told.
>
> I was released at half past one today and Mr Fraser got my clothes and gave me a blow out and some papers and sweets to go aboard …

I came aboard at 4 o'clock and now I am quite at home. I hate leaving you father but it is all for the best and God's will. It is Him I have to thank and I do from the bottom of my heart. Pray that I may walk in his way, father, and turn out an upright, truth loving man. I know that I have your forgiveness and His so I am starting a new life … if you have no objection I will remain on board for a few months … I shall write every port. Well, Dad I say goodbye and if you ever see your boy again, which I pray will happen you will see a man not a skunk …

Jack was taken on as a 'boy' for the *Marian Woodside*'s captain, James Fotheringham, with clear instructions for him throughout the voyage to be constantly at the captain's beck and call. An ordinary sailor of this period earned on average around £14 a month. Jack's pay was a miserly £1 a month.

The boy's job on a ship of this nature at the turn of the century usually entailed the lowliest tasks: helping with the cooking, cleaning the galley, serving meals to the captain, scrubbing decks, and being available in the mornings and evenings, and any other occasion that the captain required, to prepare and lay out his uniform and clothes. Besides all this, he was perpetually on call for whatever extra help might be required on deck. When the weather turned, he became a valuable extra hand to climb the rigging to furl and unfurl the sails. Nothing was too lowly for a ship's boy.

While this seeming servitude may appear harsh to us, there is little doubt that both his father and the court hoped that the experience would introduce a measure of discipline into a life that, in their judgement, had been at serious risk of 'running off the rails'.

As it turned out his 'apprenticeship' had some distinct benefits. Compared to the remainder of the crew, who in the main were older and more experienced, the physical demands made on him were not nearly as great. He was required to row the captain ashore and wait for his return when the ship called at various Pacific island ports. During these excursions he found a great deal of time to explore new places and meet new people, something most young men of his age could only dream about. To such a young man these experiences must have been exhilarating.

Jack wrote this letter to his father five days after signing on, while still in port. He asks for some towels from his school days at Cumloden.

As an example, in one of his regular letters home, and one of few that remains to chronicle this period of his life, he relates somewhat nostalgically spending two months in the port of Coquimbo in Chile seeking return cargo. He would take 'his skipper' ashore every morning, then return him for dinner much later in the evening, sometimes after the captain had wiled away his time in the port-side hostelries. Jack boasted: 'I get a better time than the men because I am ashore every day and they get one liberty day all the time we shall be in port.'

32

Life aboard a windjammer
Turning aside from the serious reasons for Jack finding himself aboard a windjammer, the experience for him was the stuff of *Boys' Own Annuals*. Windjammers were huge square-rigged sailing vessels, which at the turn of the century were contesting the coming of steam on the trading routes of the world. Clumsy to sail into the wind, they had to be 'jammed' into it, hence their name. Nevertheless, scudding before a howling Cape Horn gale or running before the trade winds they were unparalleled in their size, power and beauty.

Windjammers were awesome in every dimension, especially when compared to their lineal forebears, the wooden clipper ships. Many of them were twice as long as the clippers, yet almost as swift. They were built of iron and steel rather than wood, and herein lay their advantage. Steel bulkheads, hull plates, and even masts, made possible their great strength and size. As size and strength increased, major changes were made to hull design. Gone were the rounded sides and bottoms of earlier wooden vessels. Instead, hulls were built with straight sides and deep, flat bottoms that afforded greater cargo capacity.

Most windjammers at this time were at least 100 metres long; some reached 130 metres. The masts, a metre thick at the base, could tower as high as 60 metres above the keel, and some of the yards from which the sails were suspended were more than 30 metres long. Laid end to end, the wire and chain and manilla line of their rigging would stretch for kilometres.

As ships grew larger three masts gave away to four, even five. New rigs were developed and the ships became more manoeuvrable and manageable. Over the years windjammers came to be sailed by increasingly smaller crews. While a 1,500-tonne wooden clipper was usually sailed by a crew of 50 or 60 men, the crew of a windjammer similar to the *Marian Woodside* averaged less than 30 men. In the early 1930s, at the tail end of its era, a fully-rigged windjammer made a successful trip around the Horn with a crew of just 19.

Neither the wooden-hulled ships nor the newly emerging steel-sided steamships could carry cargoes of the size that became the windjammers' stock-in-trade. With hectares of sail on towering masts they carried thousands of tonnes of coal, guano, grain and timber

SLV 1229629

The three-masted Marian Woodside *under full sail.*
Built in Belfast in 1891, she displaced 1,475 tonnes.

around the world at impressive speeds. At the turn of the century and well into the 1920s there were hundreds of windjammers plying the oceans of the world in this type of deep-water trade.

Not unsurprisingly, life for the sailors was tough. Climbing all the way to the topmost yard-arm might take an experienced hand no more than two or three minutes. An apprentice seaman might take as long as half-an-hour. When the weather soured and the sails had to be doused in haste, seamen would go aloft to the yard and then out along it, with their feet on the footrope suspended beneath and their hands on the rail along the top of the yard, to pull and punch at the canvas to spill the air before desperate lunges to furl it.

Accidents happened frequently, but in true naval tradition sailors tended to take these for granted. All sailors were acquainted with the rule, 'One hand for the ship and one for yourself'. It was not that they were careless, but a fall from an upper yard meant almost certain death, and the wonder is that more sailors were not lost this way.

In the grand scheme of things the *Marian Woodside* was only a medium-sized, three-masted windjammer. In this first trip for Jack across the Pacific its main cargo was, Jack wrote to his father, 2,000 tonnes of coal for Coquimbo in Chile. After leaving Coquimbo, the *Marian Woodside* spent the following two months in the other ports along the Chilean coast while the captain arranged cargoes for its return to Australia. The tone of Jack's letters home at this time continued to convey his sense of obligation to the family for what he felt he had put them through; he saw his passage on the *Marian Woodside* as a chance to try and prove that, contrary to their doubts, he could take charge of his life and make something of himself.

A letter to his stepmother Elsie May dated 27 October 1910, shortly after reaching Coquimbo, attests to this:

> I thank you from the bottom of my heart for your forgiveness, mother. I have always prayed for you and Baby ever since you were married and he was born. I am sure you and I will never row again. I am more of a man now than I was when I left home and I am seventeen, nearly ...
>
> Well, dear mother you may tell father that he may rest assured about my being changed. I intend with the help of God to live a different life to what I did before. I shall not come back until I have a few pounds to give father and you ...
>
> Well about the news. We took two days short of two months to cross the briney [*sic*] and now the ship is discharging her coal. The boys are promised ten pounds and shore leave on Saturday afternoon and night if they get 600 tons out before Saturday ...
>
> Coquimbo is a nice little place with heaps of girls in it. Respectable ones I mean. I haven't quite given girls up but I don't chase them now. I have a little Spanish sweetheart already. She is coming aboard on Sunday afternoon for afternoon tea ...

Lowest of the low

In the early weeks of March 1911 Jack, having been away from Australia for close on six months, returned to Sydney on the *Marian Woodside*. However, instead of returning to Melbourne as might have been expected from the tone of his correspondence to his family, he decided to remain in Sydney, at least for the short term.

There is little doubt that Jack was a sociable and likeable young man. He made friends easily, but at the same time seems to have been a bit of a larrikin. It seems, too, that he might have been easily led, willing to take a risk and try things. He seems also to have had a streak of bravado verging on recklessness. His experiences on the *Marian Woodside* would certainly have hardened him, and perhaps encouraged him to retain his independence and savour the attractions that a boisterous and rollicking city like Sydney might offer an adventurous young man. Certainly many of the promises that he had made to his family – while most seriously meant at the time – seem to have been overtaken by the distractions and demands of the moment.

The initial weeks of his return from Chile to Sydney were tough. He retained little money from his seafaring employment, and, understandably, he did not wish to seek further support from his family. He was forced to live rough, seeking lodgings with friends and acquaintances wherever he could and eking out what money he had through frugal living.

It is not so surprising, then, that on 22 March, within only a few short weeks of leaving the *Marian Woodside*, Jack visited Gowings, a large clothing and haberdashery shop near the Sydney Town Hall, and bought a pair of shoes, a shirt and a collar using a false name. Saying that he found himself with insufficient money, he asked to return to his office to pick up money to pay for the goods. As on a previous occasion, he failed to return.

In an unrelated incident, he was arrested a few days later by the Sydney Water Police for evading a taxi fare. Again recklessly using the alias of 'Richard Raymond', he was fined in the Sydney Quarter Sessions £1/7/6, in lieu of seven days in gaol. In the meantime, however, a warrant for his arrest over his 'purchase' of goods from Gowings under false pretences had been issued. He was again arrested, and forced to appear before a judge and jury at the Sydney Quarter Sessions on the morning of 1 May 1911. He was found guilty. The following day, with his previous brushes with the law (including the failure to meet his previous special remission) now adding up, he was unsympathetically dispatched for twelve months' hard labour to Goulburn Gaol.

The twelve months Jack spent in Goulburn must have represented the low point of his life to that time. Being a seventeen-year-old in a country gaol amongst hard-bitten, long-term inmates must have been both humiliating and difficult. No letters, no reports, no family whispers of this time have survived; in fact there is no indication that his family ever knew of this episode. No doubt Jack wished it to be consigned to the dustbin of history.

With his release from Goulburn in July 1912 Jack made his way to England. Why, is a matter for conjecture. He may already have had some vague idea of joining the army; maybe he was simply looking for work again as a seaman and found himself in England. It may also have been a way of trying to put the difficulties and disappointments of his previous two years behind him. Whatever the reason for him sailing to England in 1912, it was just as likely simply a case of Jack continuing to investigate what was over the next horizon. After sending his step-mother a postcard from the busy French port of Dunkirk on 3 September of that year, he made his way to Calais the next day and joined the overnight channel boat for Dover in England.

London before the War
Jack arrived in London just two years before the declaration of World War 1, and almost two years since he had first left home. It was at the end of a summer that had been uncommonly hot, and most Britons were preoccupied with their arrangements for the coming holidays. The London 'season' was almost over, and the fashionable people who had taken part in it were in the throes of leaving town for their country estates or the smart watering places overseas. Others were settling for Brighton, Blackpool, or other popular seaside resorts for their end-of-summer break.

Early in the year of Jack's arrival the 'unsinkable' *Titanic* hit an iceberg in the North Atlantic and sank with tragic loss of life. Just prior to that the Norwegian Roald Amundsen had won the race to be the first to the South Pole (the tragic death of his competitor, Britain's Robert Scott, was still to come). In July of this same year Stockholm held the fourth Olympic Games. Significantly, however, it was also a time when 'war clouds were beginning to gather over Europe', a phrase that Jack would increasingly have seen in British newspapers and magazines.

No. **11419**   Name *John William Probert alias Lester*
alias John Leslie

Date when Portrait was taken _____ 20 - - 7 - 1910

Native place...... *Victoria*
Year of birth........ *15. 11. 93*
Arrived in) Ship......
Colony) Year.... *B.S.*
Trade or occupation) *Clerk*
previous to conviction)
Religion............ *C. of E.*
Education, degree of.... *R and W*
Height, without shoes, *5* feet *4⅜* inches
Weight) On committal. *118*
in lbs.) On discharge.
Color of hair.... *Fair*
Color of eyes .... *Blue*
Marks or special features:— *Minus*
one tooth top and one
tooth lower jaw bushy
eyebrows which meet
together

(No. of previous Portrait.................).

CONVICTIONS.

Where and When.			Offence.	Sentence.
Vic *Castlemaine P.C*	5	10	*Imposition*	*£2. or. 3 days Impt*
Water P.C	19	7	10	*Breach of influx of criminals prevention act)*	*6 mons Impt*

Jack's police record showing his imprisonment for 'Breach of influx of criminals prevention act'. (John William Probert alias Lester alias John Leslie.') The 'portrait' is dated 20/7/1910.

N°**11833**

alias *John William Probert*

Name *Richard Raymond*

alias *John Leslie*, *Lester*

Date when Portrait was taken   1 - 5 - 1911

Native place........*England*

Year of birth..........*15.11.93*

Arrived in { Ship *Marian Woodside*
Colony { Year....*1911*

Trade or occupation }
previous to conviction } *Clerk*

Religion.........*C of E*

Education, degree of........*R and W*

Height, without shoes...*5*...feet *4¾*...inches

Weight { On committal ...*128*
in lbs. { On discharge ....

Colour of hair ....*Fair*

Colour of eyes..........*Blue*

Marks or special features ....*Brown*
mole inside left
forearm. Brown mole
inside right forearm
Bushy eyebrows which
meet together

9 U 01
5 U 01

(No of previous Portrait.*1141.9*......)

G — 25-8-07.

CONVICTIONS.

Where and When.				Offence.	Sentence.
Water S.C	*28*	*3*	*11*	*Not paying cab fare*	*£1.7.6 or 7 days H.L.*
Warrants lodged	*4-4-1911*				
Sydney Q.S	*1*	*5*	*11*	*Obtaining property by false pretences and false promise*	*12 mons H.L. At the end of that time to find a surety in £50 to be of good behaviour for 12 mons in default a further 12 mons H.L.*
And 2 previous convictions for which see Photo No. as above					

A second police record, for 'Richard Raymond, alias John Leslie, alias Lester, alias John William Probert'. 'Portrait' dated 1/5/1911.

Short though it was, Jack's two years in England coincided with an extremely turbulent period, a time when the British were distracted from a great deal of what was happening elsewhere in the world, and particularly the events in Europe that were to lead to the outbreak of World War 1 – the 'Great War' – in 1914.

Nationwide strikes were threatening the country as workers struggled for the ideal of a minimum wage against an implacable Liberal government. At the same time the government was utterly confounded by the increasing energy and violence of the suffragette movement, which since 1906 had been seeking the right for women to vote. Led by Emmeline Pankhurst and her daughter Christabel, the struggle was convulsing the country. From today's viewpoint the opposition presented by the Liberals to the suffragette movement now looks almost incomprehensible, serving little else than successfully provoking its supporters to furious and passionate protest. In one of his letters home Jack comments on the turmoil he encountered in London – women battered in demonstrations, and, on hunger strikes, brutally force-fed in prison. When these measures led to loss of life, the infamous 'Cat and Mouse' Act was passed so that dangerously weakened hunger-strikers could be released and then re-arrested when strong enough to continue their sentence. In the year that Jack arrived in England, Emmeline Pankhurst went to prison on a total of twelve different occasions.

On top of all this, the government had for some time been making its way through the controversial debate over Irish home rule. Faced with a menacing show of force by the Protestant minority in the north of Ireland and a strong possibility of civil war, the government suddenly baulked and rejected home rule. Again, Britain was thrown into turmoil.

Jack spent only a short time after arriving in England before deciding what to do next. Within three weeks of his arrival he entered an Army recruitment office in London and enlisted in the First Battalion of the British Rifle Brigade. What led to his decision is speculation. Certainly is was the case that economic conditions in Britain had resulted in vast numbers of workers losing their jobs and many, as a matter of survival, joined the army. In fact in the couple of years prior to Jack's enlistment almost ninety per cent of new army recruits were men who had lost their jobs. As one contemporary writer eloquently expressed it, the drive to join the services was for many the sheer 'compulsion of destitution'.

This may also have been the case for Jack. It would be fair to assume that he had little behind him, even though a patient and forbearing father had, in one letter, promised to help him get a commission and, if necessary, provide him an allowance of £75 a year to see him through the necessary training. (At this time, with 'appropriate support' a commission in the British army could almost always be 'acquired'.) Officers were generally drawn from the traditional elites, but also from families who had newly acquired wealth from commercial or industrial ventures. For the latter, such a commission could be an entree to social position.

Some time in the three weeks between his arrival in England and enlistment as a rifleman, Jack visited the home of his grandfather, William Richard Probert, at Bures in Suffolk, even though his grandfather had died seven years previously. Perhaps he felt that he may have gained some support from his uncle, Will, an officer veteran of the Boer War and later an equerry to Princess Louise (one of Queen Victoria's daughters), to help him enter officer training and obtain a commission.

The visit to his family did not go well. Perhaps his record of misdemeanours caught up with him and his English relatives were unimpressed. In any event, a letter written to Jack's father some months later by his Uncle Will gave a less than flattering account of Jack's visit and alludes indirectly to the coldness that had arisen. Jack's father responded to the letter on 15 October 1913 with a mixture of despair and resignation:

> Claude* returned a few days before your letter arrived but he only had time to pay a hurried visit and left for Queensland so I did not get much news and that principally about my son Jack was not very cheering.

---

* Claude was half-brother to Charles, and another of Jack's uncles.

I much regret any annoyance that you may have had from him. In all letters to him I have tried to emphasise the strong admirability of his keeping quietly to himself and working hard if he wished to regain his position.

I promised him if he did so and passed his exams that I would get him a commission and was perfectly prepared to allow him up to £75 a year for a few years to see him through in spite of his doings. I believe that the offending Satan can often be whipped out of a boy by the angel of consideration.

I think he must be a bit touched in the head. He has had such a sad life. Poor boy without any mother's love ... anyhow it's up to me to see things through so far as God will permit and though things look dark I will not give up hope ...

Melbourne is very gay now. People are coming down for the Caulfield and Melbourne Cups and many, I suppose are rejoicing over the prospect of helping the poor bookie to a little more champagne and other necessaries of their existence ...

Jack returned to London, and on 23 September 1912, as a young, eighteen-year old Australian, he enlisted in the ranks of the British Rifle Brigade.

CHAPTER 3

A First Taste of War

It is strange how isolated snippets of information and observation can be retained in the memory and be forged into a picture that is later found to be very different from reality.

As youngsters we were told that Jack had served in the First World War, but we were never clear in what way. We knew he had flown in the Royal Flying Corps, and we heard exaggerated stories of the fragility and waywardness of the planes he flew. In our mother's bedroom was a framed photograph of a handsome, uniformed young man, seated in the open cockpit of a First World War aeroplane and exuding the casual confidence of a flyer.

There was also a slightly battered and well-worn chocolate tin, and, as we remember it, an old wooden cigar box suffused with the aroma of camphor, both of which held military medals and war ribbons. There were army buttons from a First World War uniform, and unrecognisable brass military insignia. It was all very confusing. Was it the army or the airforce, or perhaps both? As children we kept it simple: Jack fought in the First World War. It was some time before we discovered the full story of this period of Jack's life.

In 1996 Jack's half-brother Charles died at the age of 90. From his papers we received a number of letters and photographs that Jack had sent to his step-mother in Melbourne during the period 1910 to 1917. Much of this material was extremely useful in reconstructing other parts of this story, but of more immediate importance, there amongst the papers was a photograph we had not seen before. It was obviously a young Jack, dashingly attired in dress uniform and

Jack resplendent in his Rifle Brigade uniform, 1913.

sporting a corporal's stripe. He was standing 'at ease' outside a building, his rifle held firmly between gloved hands and on his head a squat, tufted busby bearing an indistinct silver regimental badge.

The photograph proved invaluable. It led us to discover that in September 1912 Jack had enlisted in the British army: what we were now looking at was Jack as a nineteen-year-old, attired in the green jacket of the British Rifle Brigade, at least a couple of years before the outbreak of war. We contacted the Royal Green Jackets Museum in Winchester, England, and the story of his involvement in the First World War began to gradually unfold. We confirmed Jack's enlistment in the brigade. We obtained the official history of the Rifle Brigade. We were given descriptions of barracks life and recruit training in the years before the war from the Museum's Regimental Secretary. We read the relevant annual Chronicles of the Brigade. And most importantly, we discovered the War Diaries of the First Battalion of the British Rifle Brigade.

It was like striking the jackpot. We had found a day-by-day record of the Brigade and its deployment in France and Germany, beginning before the First World War. It recorded the Battalion's final training period on the playing fields of Harrow prior to its embarkation for Le Havre, as well as the Battalion's train journey from the French coast to the war front at Le Cateau the following week. It starkly documented their march from the railway station to the village of Briastre to establish rearguard support for the British soldiers retreating from Mons. It even contained the stark statement, pencilled in at 5.30 am on 26 August 1914, 'Battle began', marking the first contact of Jack's Battalion with the advancing Germans.

With the diary we were able to trace Jack's movements. We pored over maps, located battle sites, read accounts of the actions, calculated distances, discovered names of villages and became familiar with the countryside through which his Battalion had marched and fought.

The final piece of the jigsaw for this period of Jack's life was the unexpected discovery at the Australian War Museum, in 1998, of the bibliographic and reference cards prepared on individual Australian soldiers for C.E.W. Bean's official history of Australians in the First World War. Even though he had been a member of the British army,

PRISONER OF TWO WARS

a brief record of Jack's First World War actions had been made because he was an Australian. Here we found not only confirmation of his enlistment in the Rifle Brigade, but also a very abbreviated outline of his First World War exploits. These were to become invaluable in constructing the rest of his story, as by this time we had discovered that Jack's British army personnel records had been lost in the incendiary bombing of London in 1942.

At least we now had an alternative means to unravel Jack's story.

In anticipation of war

As Jack's British army war service records were lost, the period of Jack's training and his experiences in the Rifle Brigade leading up to the World War in 1914 remain sketchy. He was sent to Meanee Barracks just outside the garrison town of Colchester, Essex. In the early months of his enlistment he applied himself with sufficient diligence to be able to proudly write home on 10 July 1913 to his step-mother boasting of his elevation to corporal in G company of the First Battalion of the Rifle Brigade. He also enclosed in his letter the wonderfully self-conscious photograph of himself resplendent in his new green Rifleman's jacket, sporting with evident pride a prominent 'Kaiser Bill' moustache. He wrote:

> I have at last got the stripe and you will note the new address ...
> Yes I received the photographs alright and am awfully pleased with them ... Mother you are getting prettier every day. What price your hat! It's a killer but it suits you down to the ground.
>
> I shall never part with the photographs as they are the only things that I have to remind me of the dear old faces I love so well. I may have been a bad boy once but I can truthfully say that I am straight at last.
>
> How I would have loved to have been with you in Torquay for I had a fairly miserable Christmas. Of course I was thinking of you and Dad far away in Australia but I feel much brighter now ...
>
> The suffragettes are playing top [billing?] in London now. Have you heard of them yet? One sees 'Vote for Women' placards up everywhere in England ...
>
> Yes dear, my moustauche [*sic*] is full grown and a regular Kaiser William too ...

46

The Rifle Brigade

The Rifle Brigade – or as it was then also known, the Prince Consort's Own – had a long and renowned history when Jack joined it. Its distinguished service stretched as far back as the Ninety-Fifth under the Duke of Wellington at the Battle of Waterloo in 1815, where, on the recommendation of the Duke, the regiment had been taken 'out of the line', styled a Brigade, and named simply after the weapon that its men had handled with such skill during the battle. It is the only instance of such a distinction being conferred on a Regiment of the British army.

From its inception the Brigade had been experimental. Its riflemen were the first to be clothed for protective cover in dark green jackets rather than the scarlet coats of other British troops of the time. They were taught to move and attack in open order to the sound of bugle horns, and were given newer, shorter rifles with far greater range and accuracy than the old smooth-bore Brown Bess muskets of the time. New and revolutionary training produced disciplined, adventurous, individual marksmen, trained to act separately and to be masters of their weapons. The riflemen's strategy was characterised by mobility, concealment and discipline, and they could create havoc when opposed to the then commonplace military strategy of most armies, which relied on deep, dense columns of soldiers. Because they worked in isolated groups and open order the Regiment carried no colours around which to rally. The role of regimental colours was replaced by individual morale and the deadly marksmanship of its riflemen All riflemen were classified as first-, second- or third-class shots, and first-class shots were rewarded with a green cockade. Hence their motto: 'Green tuffs and short barrels.'

Up to the outbreak of the First World War the Rifle Brigade served in a variety of theatres throughout the Empire. Its silver badge bore the names of almost every famous battle in the previous hundred years of British military history. Its famous campaigns – on the North West Frontier, in Afghanistan, the African Veldt, the deserts of Sudan and Egypt – had contributed to the rich tradition of the Brigade that Jack joined in that September of 1912.

The Rifle Brigade no longer exists, but its history and legacy continues, embodied in the famous regiment now known as the Royal Green Jackets.

Outbreak of war

When they first learned that their country was at war the immediate emotion experienced by most British was probably surprise. The assassination of an obscure Austrian archduke in the Balkans in June 1914 had led to much sabre-rattling among the Continental powers, making war in Europe virtually inevitable. However, in the months leading up to its declaration Britain was still far more engrossed with the possibility of civil war in Ireland, and it was not until Belgium's neutrality was violated by Germany's invasion that, on 4 August, Britain finally declared war.

Spirited patriotism gave rise to rapid mobilisation. British citizens believed that they had a good and noble cause, and large numbers of men rushed to join the force. (Many had also joined just prior to the outbreak of war because of economic difficulties.) Thousands anxious not to miss the war – and expecting it to be over by Christmas – formed long queues outside recruiting offices. Some even saw it as an opportunity for a short holiday from the humdrum of everyday existence. Many, influenced by friends and work colleagues, joined up in groups, leading to what became known as 'pals' battalions. They were recruited in large numbers from workplaces and sports and social clubs. Little did they appreciate the consequences of this mass enlistment, which were brought home when hundreds of thousands of men were annihilated in the bloodbath of the Western Front in the years to follow.

A typical story records that one lad enlisted in an alcoholic haze after seeing a friend off to the front. He never remembered 'taking the shilling', and when the sergeant came next morning and claimed him, he was as surprised as his wife was annoyed!

The opening shots

From the outset the German strategy misled the French into believing that the main German attack was to be through Alsace-Lorraine on France's north-eastern border, when instead they pushed their main forces into Belgium and northern France for a direct attack on Paris. Initially the strategy worked well. The French rushed the select of their army to meet the attack from Alsace-Lorraine, suffering heavy casualties when the Germans' First and Second Armies swept down through Belgium and into France. The Germans drove both the French and the newly arrived British Expeditionary Forces (dubbed a 'contemptible little army' by Kaiser Wilhelm, Supreme Commander of the German army) before them. However, the Allies fought more effectively than the German command had anticipated, and the German advance was gradually slowed to a point where the Allies were able to mount an effective series of rearguard actions, driving the Germans back on themselves and behind the River Aisne.

By the end of 1914 the armies had discovered the relentless power of artillery, which forced them into trench warfare, and the machine-gun and rifle fire that made 'over-the-top' attacks so costly. Moreover, the efficiency with which reinforcements could be rushed by either side to stem breakthroughs continually undermined the most promising of offensives.

A stalemate ensued, and the Western Front – as it was soon called – became, as it were, the central stage of the war for close to four years, and a graveyard for hundreds of thousands of young men who were to die in futile efforts to breach each other's defences.

The first British Expeditionary Force

At the outbreak of war four of the six available divisions of the British Expeditionary Forces were quickly mobilised, and crossed to France between 12 and 17 August. (The British First Corps comprised the First and Second Divisions under General Haig, while the Second Corps was made up of the Third and Fifth Divisions under General Dorrien-Smith.) Their Supreme Commander, Sir John French, received orders to co-operate with the French as an independent commander, but was instructed by the Government to be extremely cautious in exposing his small force to danger and losses. It was agreed that the British divisions would move quickly to Soignes, where they would take up a position on the flanks of the French and prepare for a joint move to the outskirts of the small town of Mons, in what was anticipated to be the first British engagement with the enemy.

For some reason the departure from England of the Fourth Division, of which Jack's First Battalion of the Rifle Brigade was a part, was delayed. The Battalion had been in barracks at Colchester on 4 August when mobilisation orders were given by the War Office. Within four days their mobilisation was complete. Another week was devoted to intensive training before, on 17 August, they joined the other elements of the Fourth Division on the famous playing fields of the old Harrow School. Here they spent their final three days of preparation, before joining the train for Southampton.

On 22 August Jack embarked on the SS *Cestrian*, and the following day his Brigade – comprising 24 officers and 964 other ranks – reached Le Havre. The troops landed and made their way through the centre of the town, and by the middle of the afternoon were camped on a prepared site on the heights just above the town, ready for their next step. An interesting aside in the Brigade's official history refers to the help received from the local Boy Scouts, who acted as guides and unofficial interpreters for the newly arrived British troops.

Meanwhile, in the week prior to the arrival of the Fourth Division in France the main British Expeditionary Force (BEF) had moved inland and begun to concentrate itself between Maubeuge and Le Cateau. On 20 August, just as the German troops were entering Brussels and approaching Namur, General Joffre, the French commander, decided on a combined advance in which the BEF was now to join with the western flank of the French Fifth Army and move towards Soignes near Nivelles. Sir John French ordered the British to occupy, by 23 August, a line a kilometre or so in front of the town of Mons, running roughly north-west to south-east, and creating a total Allied front almost 27 kilometres in length.

In the three weeks since 4 August, and before the arrival of the British at Mons, the western flank of the German army had moved rapidly along the Dutch border and marched into Belgium through the streets of Aachen. Day and night German columns had poured west, before wheeling to the south-west from the level of Brussels. In fifteen days marching the German First Army under von Kluck covered nearly 290 kilometres, with the intention of establishing their line as quickly as possible from Amiens, La Fère and Rethel to Thionville. Von Kluck knew that the British Expeditionary Force had already landed in Belgium, but as he approached Mons he still believed it to be somewhere near Tournai, a small village 50 kilometres north-west of his present position. Instead, in the early morning light of 23 August, he found directly in front of him and alongside the French the divisions of the newly arrived British forces, dug in and well prepared for what was to be their first military encounter of the Great War.

The battle of Mons

The British troops found protection behind the canal where it curved north and east around the town. They took up positions amongst the scattered chimneys and black shale-heaps and behind the pit-heads of what was a large and ugly expanse of coalfields.

23 August was a Sunday. At first light a fine summer mist covered the ground, and within a couple of hours light rain began to fall. The bells of the local churches rang out rather incongruously as the people of the town and surrounding small hamlets made their way to Mass, unaware of what was to come.

At this stage von Kluck could have easily outflanked the British – with his superior numbers it would probably have been disastrous for the British if he had. (In total, about 70,000 British troops with 300 guns faced some 160,000 Germans with 600.) Luckily for the British, von Kluck had been placed under the control of von Bulow, the commander of the German Second Army; orders had been given for his troops to remain in close touch with the Second, and they were absolutely forbidden to swing wide. So von Kluck came directly at the British like a bull with its head down.

Close to nine o'clock the Germans came down the road towards the canal bridges singing their marching songs. They wore field-grey uniforms, jackboots and black helmets with tall spikes, but the helmets and their ornate front badges were hidden under grey cloth covers. The British (many with the favoured heavy 'Old Bill' moustache) wore rough khaki serge with long puttees and flat-topped, peaked caps.

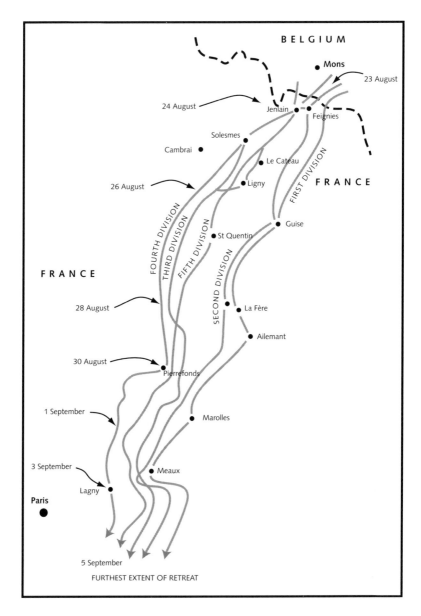

The British retreat from Mons, 23 August–5 September 1914.

From rough trenches along the canal bank, houses and the slopes of the slag-heaps, the British opened rapid rifle fire. The Germans maintained their march, but the rifle fire scythed the solid ranks of oncoming soldiers. Fifteen aimed shots to the minute was the British norm, and later, the Germans who survived the initial onslaught found it difficult to believe that they had been held up simply by rifle fire. For a long time they believed they had faced a 'machine-gun army', but, like themselves, the British had in fact only two machine-guns per battalion. It was rapid fire like no mass conscript army could produce. At that range the bullets' trajectory was flat, and with the Germans' dense formation some bullets went through two or three men before expending their force. Grey corpses piled up on the road, along the canal bank and in the fields. The light rain stopped and the sun came out. The Germans re-formed and came on, second and third waves forming behind the first before the advance was brought to a stop.

However, it was only a temporary halt to the powerful German onslaught. In a number of places the German forces began to make inroads, and by late afternoon it was clear to the Allied commanders that the superior forces of the Germans were just too strong to hold. The British had suffered severe losses and needed to withdraw. The French, too, had been heavily engaged. By nightfall the British had fallen back from Mons, and by dawn of the following day the British, with the First Corps on the right and the Second Corps on the left, were left holding a line about five kilometres south of Mons. Conforming with the movements of the French on his right, Sir John French gave orders for a further thirteen kilometre retreat to an east-west line stretching from Longueville through to Bavai. The British fell back to this position, constantly harassed.

This was the beginning of a long retreat for the British and French forces, which continued for thirteen days and subjected these troops to a march of almost 250 kilometres under duress.

The retreat from Mons

The Forest of Mormal lay directly in the path of the British retreat. Believing that roads through the forest were impassable, the two

British corps split to pass on either side. In the early morning of 26 August the advancing Germans harassed both corps. The First British Corps, led by General Douglas Haig, was involved in an inconclusive skirmish from which it escaped relatively unscathed. The other battle, against the Second Corps, was deliberately forced by the British general, Smith-Dorrien, who realised that if the retreat was not to become a rout he had to stand his ground and strike his pursuers as hard as possible before he could safely resume his retreat under cover of their discomfiture. Le Cateau was the site for this stand.

Jack's first battle encounter

On Monday evening, 24 August, Jack's First Battalion of the Rifle Brigade was preparing to entrain at Le Havre. The first battle for the British in the Great War had been fought, and they were already in retreat. In the early hours of the following morning his Battalion's train rumbled slowly through Rouen and then Amiens, before grinding to a halt at around five o'clock on Tuesday, 25 August. The First Battalion had reached the forward area.

Men stuck their head out through the windows and saw the name Le Cateau. It meant nothing to them. An anxious staff officer hurried up to the Battalion's commanding officer and gave orders, which were quickly taken down by candlelight. Only in the bustle of getting off the train did the troops realise they had actually reached the front, and both the enemy and the retreating British were only a matter of a few kilometres away.

The battle of Mons had just concluded. That they were now in a war zone was emphasised after they had marched clear of the station and the map boxes were hurriedly unpacked. They discovered that the contents of the boxes consisted almost exclusively of maps of Belgium!

Jack's Battalion marched through Le Cateau, and proceeded through Neuvilly to Briastre, where it rejoined the 11th Infantry Brigade. The march was hot and tiring, with no time for rest. As soon as they reached Briastre two companies were detailed to dig in north of the village. The remaining companies of the Battalion settled in near a farmhouse at the northern end of the village, next to the light railway at the road fork. During the march from Le Cateau they had engaged an enemy aeroplane with their rifles – the first shots fired by the regiment in this theatre of war. Curiously, the First Battalion marched into this, its first action in the Great War, on its regimental birthday.

The overall task of the newly arrived Fourth Division, most of which was now in the forward area, was to provide rearguard support to the retreating Second Corps, who were still moving to a position where they intended to make their stand against the advancing Germans. The Second Corps' line was beginning to form, and its eastern flank was resting in Le Cateau, which ultimately gave its name to the battle.

The day passed quietly enough for Jack's Battalion, with a steady stream of the remnants of the Second Corps' troops moving through his position, most of whom were looking to rejoin their detachments.

The appearance of the retreating troops amply demonstrated what they had been through. Most had been on the move without a break since dawn two days before the Mons battle, fighting, entrenching and marching. A few fleeting words snatched as they passed gave only some idea of what was to follow.

The Fourth Division was instructed to hold its line against the Germans until the last of the retreating troops were through. Only then was Jack's Battalion to fall back and re-establish itself in the rear, in a line stretching from Fontaine-au-pire to near Wambaix.

By the late afternoon of 25 August the last of the Second Corps troops had finally passed and the time came for the fall-back to the new line. It rapidly became a nightmare. A heavy thunderstorm broke, and the downpour and the heavy volume of traffic combined to convert the road into a quagmire. Nevertheless by two o'clock in the early morning of 26 August the main body of Jack's Battalion had settled to the north-west of Fontaine-au-pire, on the road that ran down the slope towards Cattenières. Men found spots for themselves wherever they could on either side of the track and snatched what sleep they could. Orders were given to the Battalion to hold its ground till the morning.

In the dawn light of 26 August the men of the First Battalion

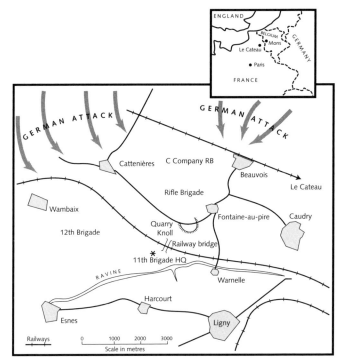

First Battalion rearguard action at Quarry Knoll, 26 August 1914

could now see for themselves the cultivated fields that surrounded them, and the gradual slope that fell away towards the village of Fontaine-au-pire. However, they also saw themselves facing an advancing body of German cavalry and artillery. While the cavalry were initially driven back, the superior numbers of German infantry forced the Battalion to retreat.

What followed must have been a remarkable sight. The accepted standards of 1914 forebade a retirement at any pace other than a disdainful walk. Ground was being given up: the enemy must be clearly shown that no pressure of his was the cause. An eye-witness noted:

> The Battalion received orders to retire which it did almost as though it was a drill movement on parade, one company walking back in line for a couple of hundred yards, while the others covered it with fire; and then the other moving back. It was all done steadily at a walk; there was no running about at all.

Jack's wounding

At the end of this rearguard action the Battalion took up its fall-back position in a sunken road that ran roughly east-west across the Quarry Knoll and parallel to the railway. At this stage the First Battalion was slightly to the rear of the overall fighting line of the Fourth Division, but the pressure from the enemy so increased in the following hours that their position quickly turned into a frontline trench. The deadly rapid fire of the Riflemen helped them to hold their position, and even when the German line was reinforced and its infantrymen made a determined effort to advance the withering fire of the Riflemen repulsed them.

As the day wore on the bombardment from the German artillery steadily increased, and the necessity both for cover and the thinning out of the line to neutralise the effects of shrapnel was realised by officers and men alike. The forward position held by the companies of the First Battalion was heavily fired upon from both flanks by German infantry. Nevertheless the Germans were still unprepared to risk a rush on the resolute riflemen, who maintained deadly fire. Instead the German soldiers crept in on all sides until they were within a hundred metres of the British.

The British risked complete encirclement. Already the enemy had crossed the railway embankment on both flanks, and but for a gap of about four hundred metres the detachment was surrounded. To stay longer would have been a useless waste of men. However, it was also clear that any attempt to retire from the firing line as an organised body of troops would result in annihilation. A medical officer volunteered to stay with the seriously wounded who were unable to be moved, and the remainder of the riflemen retreated to Ligny at top speed, with every man for himself.

The losses in Jack's First Battalion on 26 August amounted to eight officers and 350 other ranks, almost forty per cent of the troops who had left Southampton just three days earlier. By evening of the same day, when orders were given for the retreat from Ligny a mere 200 Riflemen from the First Battalion marched away.

The battle of Le Cateau resulted in a total of over 8,000 casualties. From the available evidence Jack was wounded in the arm and leg some time during the fighting along the sunken road near Fontaine-au-pire. On the same day he also won a Military Medal for bravery, but as happened for so many acts of bravery, in the heat and confusion of battle no citation appears to have been written to inform the event (see Appendix 1). As a result of his injuries Jack was captured in the Cathedral at Ligny (which had become a temporary military hospital for Allied wounded) when the town was over-run by Germans late in the evening of 26 August. Along with the hundreds of others wounded and captured at Le Cateau, Jack became a German prisoner of war.

Continuing the retreat

At three o'clock in the afternoon of 26 August, when the sheer weight of the German divisions had begun to tell, a decision for general retirement was made by General Smith-Dorrien. Throughout the late afternoon and far into the night, despite the intense exhaustion of the troops and the congestion and confusion in the lines, the British continued to retreat.

The British reached safety near Paris and behind the Aisne on 6 September. By this time the Germans had become stretched by the speed of their advance since 4 August. Weakened by the diversion of troops to the Eastern front to contain the Russians, they now suddenly found themselves on the receiving end of a major counterattack mounted by the rejuvenated French. From 5 to 12 September the Germans were determinedly driven back to the Marne, where the protagonists were to remain in relentless and bloody trench warfare for nearly four years.

The war of movement was over; instead, years of grinding mud, bloodshed and indescribable horror lay ahead.

CHAPTER 4

Black Bread and Barbed Wire

In its pursuit of the Allies after the Battles of Mons and Le Cateau the German army swept through the small French town of Ligny. Hundreds of wounded Allied troops had sought refuge in the small public buildings scattered through the town. Jack was confined to a palliasse on the floor of the cathedral with shrapnel wounds to his leg and arm when the Germans took him prisoner.

The days that followed were filled with uncertainty and boredom. None of the prisoners knew what would happen, and the hours inside the church passed monotonously. There was little respite, apart from a couple of young, overworked German doctors who appeared regularly to provide morphia and direct orderlies on dressing the wounds of the more seriously injured men. The captives were otherwise left largely to fend for themselves, and instructed not to move beyond the confines of the building.

In the middle of each day and again in the evening, the guards brought the men bowls of thin watery soup and loaves of black, doughy, almost indigestible bread. This was followed with a milkless and sugarless acorn coffee, ladled from large tin pannikins and served by those men less restricted by their wounds.

On their fourth day of capture, the German guards unexpectedly entered the church and instructed all those who could walk to assemble outside and march the short distance to the town's railway station. Those who had difficulty in reaching the station under their own power were to be supported by their fellow prisoners, while those unable to walk were to be ferried on the backs of trucks and open carts commandeered from the local townspeople.

By the time the prisoners reached the station Jack's group had been joined by hundreds of other captured British, French and Belgians. They were herded down a long, grey asphalt platform to a line of filthy cattle trucks, fitted with heavy sliding doors in the centre and small elevated trapdoors high on either side. With around 50 other young British, Jack was unceremoniously bundled inside.

At this early stage their captors were beginning to make ominous distinctions between their prisoners. Whereas 20 Belgians were loaded to a truck and straw scattered on the floor, the British found themselves in groups of over 50, crushed into their trucks with neither straw nor provision for sanitation. To further emphasise the distinctions the Germans scrawled in chalk on the exterior of the trucks: *'Belgian gut, Franzosen gut, aber English Schwein'* ('Belgians are OK, the French are OK, but the English are pigs').

The journey into Germany

Jack's initial destination was Braunschweig, an industrial and commercial city in Lower Saxony a little over 880 kilometres away and not far from the German capital, Berlin. The insides of the trucks were dark and dirty and the air grew more fetid as the hours passed. While the wounded were found places to lie, most of the men were forced to stand for long periods of time, taking turns to crouch on the floor of the truck with their legs pulled up tightly into their stomach, leaning against one another back to back.

Throughout the first night and the next day they received nothing to eat or drink, nor were they allowed out of the trucks. Only late on the second night of their journey, while the train remained overnight in a siding, were the men supplied their first meal, a ration of sour black bread and yellowish, warm soup.

On a couple of occasions during the long, cold journey into Germany, the train pulled up at small stations, and the heavy sliding doors of the trucks would burst open for the men to be confronted by German soldiers scavenging warm outer clothing to help combat the biting cold of the night.

*Postcard Jack sent home to tell of his wounding and
hospitalisation in a converted restaurant. The 'x' on the
front marks where his bed was.*

On the evening of the third day of their journey they finally
arrived in Braunschweig, and Jack and some other wounded soldiers
were detrained. Met by a small group of Red Cross volunteers who
supplied them with a welcome ration of hot soup and bread, they
were taken by truck to a military hospital a short distance from the
station. The men soon discovered that the place chosen for their
convalescence had been a popular restaurant called 'Holst's Garden';

only a few hours before their arrival it had been rapidly converted to a temporary military hospital.

It was just two weeks since Jack had left England. He was at last able to send a postcard to his parents letting them know that he had been captured and held as a prisoner of war in Braunschweig, but that he was safe and sound, at least at this stage. In deference to the brevity demanded by the prevailing censorship he simply told his parents: 'I was captured when wounded. I am now nearly recovered.' He relayed no further details, and, perhaps as an afterthought, on the picture side of the obviously pre-war postcard of the restaurant Jack drew a pencilled cross to show his parents his exact bed location in the converted restaurant.

Jack remained in convalescence in Braunschweig for a little over three weeks before completing the final part of his journey east. It was just a short trip of about 80 kilometres to Döberitz, a town 27 kilometres south-west of Berlin, where he was to spend the next three years as a prisoner of war of the Germans.

Recreating Döberitz

Promising leads can so easily dissolve into dead ends. At first the search for information about Jack's three years in Döberitz proved to be just such a case. For example, lengthy correspondence with the Comité International de la Croix-Rouge (the Red Cross) in Geneva requesting a search of their Central Tracing Agency archives for information proved largely negative. We also wrote to the Dutch National Archives seeking background material on Döberitz. (The Netherlands had acted as the protecting power for British prisoners in Germany, and Dutch diplomatic staff carried out hundreds of camp visits during this time.) Again, the search was to no avail, and little information about Jack or the camp was forthcoming.

Our greatest disappointment was the result of a search through European libraries and archives for a magazine called *The Link*, published irregularly in Döberitz by the British prisoners. But after twelve months of frustration, we finally obtained a filmed copy of the magazine from the British Museum. It contains a couple of literary efforts quite unrelated to camp life, some nostalgic reminiscences of home by the editors, some jokes and repartee about camp life that had unfortunately lost much of their meaning with the passing of the years, and some pen-and-ink drawings of camp personalities by a talented camp artist. It was a fascinating document insofar as it was an example of the activities allowed prisoners in Döberitz, but unfortunately it provided us with little of the contextual information we needed to illuminate life in that particular German prison.

In the end the most relevant sources of information for this part of the story were a small number of cards and letters written by Jack from the camp, and a fading, yellowed copy of an article published on 3 December 1938 in the *Sydney Morning Herald*, which we discovered amongst our mother's personal papers. The article, written by Geoffrey Whitlock, described in detail his three attempts to escape from the Döberitz camp. The first attempt was with Jack, and this first-hand account of one of Jack's adventures proved invaluable.

Early days in Döberitz

During the course of the Great War the Germans captured nearly 2,800,000 prisoners, most of whom were interned in over 150 POW camps scattered throughout Germany. Döberitz held two of these camps. Separated by a wide gravel road, each camp was surrounded by high, electrified, barbed-wire fences, with machine-gun posts at regular intervals around the perimeter. The two camps sat high on a hill overlooking Döberitz, dubbed Hungry Hill for reasons that became quickly evident to the train-loads of prisoners who began arriving in the early weeks of September 1914.

The No. 1 camp initially held around 4,000 men, mainly those captured in late August 1914 during the Mons and Le Cateau battles. The second camp held an overflow of another 400 men, and was distinguished from the first by its tents. By early November a further 3,000 Russians captured on the Eastern front joined the 'Mons men'. This severely tested camp conditions, which had already begun to deteriorate.

Jack arrived in the camp just at this time. Like the prisoners before him he found his personal letters, photos and notebooks confiscated, and money he still held changed into German coinage. He was left

THE SUBTERRINE.

A pen-and-ink drawing from the POW camp magazine, The Link, *produced by prisoners during their internment in Döberitz.*

with his summer military uniform, which would soon prove distressingly inappropriate for the harsh German winter.

Jack was allocated to an austere, wooden hut in the No. 1 camp. The hut was so crowded that men were forced to sleep on the floor, three men sharing a mattress. Some were even forced to take their blankets and sleep in the open lobby of their hut, through one of Germany's bitterest winters.

These early days in Döberitz were harsh and demanding. Prisoners were only issued with bowls and spoons; knives were confiscated. The men sharpened their spoons on stones to help them divide their daily 1.5 kg loaves of bread which, along with soup and coffee, became their staple diet for the next few months.

This diet created early and serious problems for both the men and the camp authorities. Established with typical German efficiency, the daily routine meant that the men were given coffee as early as six o'clock in the morning. At noon, soup and loaves of doughy, black bread were distributed, and at six in the evening the men received coffee and ate what remained of the day's bread ration. It was not long before this inadequate diet led to men collapsing, and it so weakened bladders that many were having to make latrine visits at all times of the day and night. The Germans were forced to make extensive changes to the diet.

By the time the Russians swelled the camp numbers in November, both camps had become infested with vermin. Men began to suffer badly from rashes, which some scratched till they were raw with red, seeping sores. There were no washing or bathing facilities, and only two taps were available for the 4,000 prisoners, who were forced to carry out their ablutions in the open, with soup bowls as their only utensils. But by the end of 1914 and after three months in camp, conditions began slowly to improve. A number of huts with tarred felt exteriors were erected by the prisoners, reducing the pressure on accommodation and allowing the tents in the No. 2 camp to be removed. Pumps and wooden troughs were also provided for washing and bathing.

One of the more serious problems in these early days of the camp was the German order that the Russians share huts with the British.

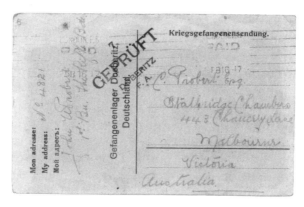

A postcard sent by Jack from Döberitz on New Year's Eve, 1916: left, the reverse of the postcard shown at top. Postcards were written in pencil for censorship purposes. Right, a photograph postcard, now much deteriorated. It is dated 12 June 1917.

This led to rancorous friction. The British argued that the Russians made no attempt to maintain elementary standards of hygiene and that their body odour combined with their practice of keeping their windows closed at all times made the huts uninhabitable. As the problem festered there was constant bickering, and at times outright physical assault. By December the camp authorities, who had begun shipping out prisoners to work at sites around Germany, took advantage of the opportunity to reorganise the camp's accommodation. Prisoners were reallocated to new barracks, and mostly placed with men from the same regiment or country. A marked change immediately occurred in the atmosphere and morale of the camp.

Nevertheless time hung heavily for the prisoners in these early months. At first almost no work was available, only a few general tasks like cleaning the guards' barracks, washing refuse bins and, for those with building skills, some construction of additional barracks and amenities.

In the early part of 1915 the war began to create serious manpower difficulties for the Germans. The demand for able-bodied men for the Front meant serious shortages of labour occurred throughout the country in factories, mines and farms. The authorities decided to use their POW resources to make up the shortfall. Thus many of the POWs found themselves in industrial plants as labourers or working in the fields as farmhands. The men from Döberitz were soon marching out of camp each morning to work in the nearby suburb at jobs allocated to them by the Corporation of Hohenschonhausen, or to spend the day working on nearby farms. As a consequence, life for those who worked outside the camp improved markedly. Not only did it bring about a change of environment and morale for the prisoners, it alleviated the monotony of camp and made life just a little more bearable.

Letters home
In the early months of 1915 another significant boost to camp morale occurred when POWs were given permission to write and receive mail. Prisoners were allowed to send two letters and four postcards a month, with no restriction on the quantity of correspondence

received. However strict limitations were laid down as to what could be written. Neither pen nor indelible pencil was permitted. Only lead pencil was allowed, enabling the censors to erase anything to which they took exception. (For a long time while piecing together this part of the story we had wondered why postcards Jack sent home from Döberitz were all written in pencil!)

Official stationery was issued for letters and postcards, and as the camp became better organised a small stock was carried by each barracks' post office to meet the needs of its residents. As the postal system developed postmen were appointed from amongst the prisoners to collect and distribute the mail, and later, when pillar boxes were established in each of the barracks, elected postmen duly cleared the boxes, recorded the mail and held it for ten days before forwarding. This bizarre retention was claimed to be for military purposes, though the protocol appears to have been neither understood nor appreciated by the men of either side.

More often than not there were frustrating delays of anything up to three months, with mail having to pass first through censors, then the Red Cross in Switzerland, and, in Jack's case, being routed via England before being relayed to his parents and friends in Melbourne. Nevertheless his correspondence was regular, and while expressing frustration with the irregular arrival of mail, the few postcards that have survived are generally infused with optimism and hope. A letter, for instance, to his young half-brother Charles in the middle of 1915, three years before the end of the war, contained a promise he would be home, 'to pick apples [by] next summer'.

Not unexpectedly, interruptions to camp correspondence would occasionally occur, which led to some rather creative remedies by prisoners. In one camp the men quickly discovered that letters passed rapidly through the system if they were addressed to someone of unusual rank. Those to the Duchess of Brighton, for example, (but with the family member's correct address), always seemed to reach their destination with remarkable speed.

One poor Russian in Döberitz wanted 100 marks very badly, so he wrote a letter to God. Naturally, the letter had to be censored, but the sympathetic censor and friends to whom he showed it decided to make a collection; by return post they sent the 50 marks they collected. The Almighty, it is said, promptly received another letter telling him that it was *100* marks and would he be kind enough to send the remaining 50 without delay!

Food parcels

Along with the opportunity for letter writing, camp authorities also eventually gave permission for parcels of food and clothing to enter the camp. Later in the war, as the Germans experienced severe food shortages and supplies to many of the POW camps dwindled, both the camp administration and the prisoners came to rely more and more on these food parcels. Some idea of the size of the parcel shipment to Germany can be gathered from the fact that at Camp Munster, where over 30,000 Allied prisoners were held, a total of 240,000 food parcels arrived during May 1916 alone. This was an average of almost eight parcels per man per month, which kept a post office staff of over 220 fully employed.

At the beginning of the war food and clothing relief was the responsibility of separate Red Cross organisations in each of the Allied countries. There was no centralisation. So British prisoners like Jack received parcels directly from their relatives, from various regimental societies, and even from their 'godmothers' – charitable women who made it a practice to send parcels to British prisoners whose names they had secured from local regimental committees. Not unexpectedly, abuses of the latter occurred – addresses of 'godmothers' were sometimes traded among the prisoners, the market price of the address being determined by the quality of parcels received. Some prisoners received as many as twenty parcels a month from different godmothers, and would auction or sell their contents to less fortunate fellow prisoners.

As soon as parcels began to arrive in Döberitz in early 1915 camp life improved immensely, evidenced by the photographs Jack sent home to his parents. In their early letters men requested mainly food, tobacco and clothing. Warm clothing and boots were at a premium, as the Germans supplied only those in desperate need with replacement clothes. In Jack's surviving letter-cards to his parents there are

Postcards of Jack, identified with an 'x', with fellow prisoners in Döberitz.
Left, 23 January 1917; right, marked 'Rec^d 24/6/16'.

regular requests for things like boots, waistcoats and chocolate. There were equally frequent expressions of extreme gratitude for the arrival of each parcel.

Day-to-day life in camp

The quality of life in German POW camps varied considerably. Many of the camps were requisitioned public facilities, hurriedly converted into POW camps to accommodate the surge of prisoners from the war front.

Gutersloh had been an unused lunatic asylum, Colberg a sanatorium built over thermal springs in a picturesque valley covered with forest. Some camps were established for commissioned officers, others like Ruhleben were used for foreigners who, unfortunately caught in Germany at the outbreak of war, had been interned as aliens.

While directly responsible to the central German POW Camp Directorate, individual camp commanders were given considerable latitude in running their camps. Hence there were substantial differences not only in the amenities provided but also in the way the camps were administered and organised. Regular visits by Red Cross and YMCA representatives helped to ensure reasonable standards in most prisons, and representations to camp commanders generally led to useful changes in most camps.

In his book *In the Prison Camps of Germany* Charles Hoffman, a YMCA representative, describes how in the Ruhleben camp

> on going on the rounds ... one was surprised to find an historical club, a science club, a music club, two or three theatrical societies, and the like. One of the main thoroughfares between two of the barracks was known as Bond Street. Here were shops of the most varied type where one could purchase everything from cooking utensils and toilet articles to clothing and books. A shoe shop and a tailor shop were also to be found. Most unique was the camp police force made up of British prisoners of war who were responsible for the maintenance of order and the prevention of thieving in the camp ...
>
> The Grandstand University so named because of its origins underneath the grandstand where the first classes were held had grown to large proportions, with faculty and students and catalogues of courses ... many a prisoner prepared himself and passed the entrance examinations for Oxford University ...
>
> (*In the Prison Camps of Germany*, p. 45)

Big camps like Gutersloh and Crefeld even had large and very good orchestras and choirs. Camps differed enormously in size and the quality of their administration, but it appears from brief references in Hoffman's book that at Döberitz a number of sporting, social and recreational opportunities had been established for the men. The camp magazine, *The Link*, was published by the prisoners on at least four occasions. Not only was it sent home to the families of the prisoners, but it was also widely distributed through many of the other German POW camps.

On most days in Döberitz there were British games like football and boxing to watch and play. A games committee was established in the early part of 1915 to fill the days with as many activities and

Group photo of Döberitz POWs, Jack again identifying himself with an 'x'.

interests as possible. International games, inter-barracks contests and
games between officers and orderlies were regularly played with great
keenness – and even occasioned a small amount of betting.

During his time in Döberitz Jack devoted a great deal of time to
learning German, and later, possibly due to his newly acquired fluency
in the language, he became a camp representative for the Red Cross.
(During World 2 War fellow prisoners of war claimed that Jack told
them he was even set up by the Germans in separate accommodation
in Berlin to carry out liaison tasks required by his new position. There
is only anecdotal evidence, however, to support this – on the balance
of probabilities the story has probably been somewhat distorted by
the passage of time.)

Escape bids

In their early days of captivity prisoners' breaks for freedom were more often than not spur-of-the-moment efforts, without plan or support. Perimeter wire would be cut or clambered over, or men allocated jobs outside the camp might make a dash for freedom when an appropriate moment arrived. However, most men were recaptured either because their deficiency in the German language gave them away, or their limited knowledge of the countryside and appropriate escape routes left them easy prey for searchers.

As the war wore on the Germans made substantial improvements in the containment of their prisoners by bringing in extra sentries and, later, making rigorous and unexpected searches for maps, compasses, food and escape kits. They gradually strengthened the outer perimeter of most camps with arc lights and increased the number of machine-gun posts. At one camp, Schwarmstedt, dogs were introduced to both discourage escapes and track down those who did. However, one dog was found to be open to corruption when he realised that camp prisoners could provide him with better and more plentiful food than his masters. So corrupted did the dog become that it is claimed that when one of the men actually escaped, he took the dog along with him!

However, the changes made by camp authorities did little to diminish the prisoners' hopes of escape. 'How to bolt' and 'when to bolt' were favoured themes of discussion in the privacy of the barracks. And there was no end of imaginative and daring escape plans hatched. It became a routine of prison life for men to keep their eyes and ears open, and regularly appraise the lie of the land in case an opportunity presented itself. Over time, escape kits of money, clothes and food were carefully assembled and stashed in secret places, ready for use whenever an opportunity might present itself.

Rules for escape also gradually evolved. For example, it was understood that if two prisoners were to escape together they were as far as humanly possible to stay with each other, but each was always to act in accordance with the first law of escape – self-preservation. If, for instance, one was wounded by a shot or met with an incapacitating accident, his comrade was not to stop and render assistance. Interestingly, the spirit of this rule was later to save Jack.

Some escapes were more barefaced than others. In one camp two British prisoners dressed as French orderlies marched solemnly to an empty sentry box in the camp, laid it flat, placed their escape kits inside and carried it to the entrance of the camp. There they informed the guard that they were under instructions to move the sentry box outside the wire. The guard went inside to check their story, and was utterly flummoxed to find on his return that the two men had vanished. He was left to ignominiously return the sentry box to its proper place, and contemplate the wrath of his camp commander.

Another enterprising young prisoner stole a German officer's uniform and, suitably disguised by an artist friend, unlocked the main gate with a homemade key. Under the eyes of the whole camp he casually walked to freedom with his swagger stick neatly tucked under his arm.

Apart from such spirited – and perhaps apocryphal – bids for freedom, prisoners constantly made careful escape plans. Maps of the countryside were sought and then lent to others to copy. The thin paper found in Huntly and Palmer biscuit tins which arrived in food parcels was eagerly sought after for tracing multiple copies of maps. Compasses, too, were home-made from magnets, needles and old watch cases scrounged around the camp. In one camp the Germans actually allowed the purchase of civilian hats and rucksacks from the canteen: when the latter were bought up too quickly by the prisoners the Germans wisely refused to order more.

Saving food for escapes was a more difficult task. Tins and packets sent in relief parcels were generally required to be kept in the parcel office and opened by the prisoners only in the office under the supervision of staff. However, unopened tins could occasionally be slipped into pockets when visiting the parcel office, and escape kits were gradually supplemented over time.

In some camps the disillusionment of guards could sometimes be turned to advantage, leading to the acquisition of many useful items for escape kits. Sentries frequently became fed up with their long hours of duty, extremely poor food and the severe punishment they received if negligence was proved against them. Judicious bribery in the shape of a small tin of meat or bar of soap could obtain a wide range of requisites.

Desperate news from home

In a postcard sent by Jack to his step-mother in the third week of April, 1917 the first hint emerged that Jack thought his father might be seriously ill. An earlier letter from a friend had pointed out that his father did not seem to be 'as fit as usual'. Desperately frustrated by his inability to do anything, Jack wrote immediately to find out what was wrong, but it was a frustrating five months before he received a reply from his step-mother and discovered the seriousness of his father's throat cancer. Jack was distraught:

> My poor darling mother I have only just received your card of 20th May. Oh Lord what a shock. I am writing in disjointed sentences. I can't fix my mind. You know my feelings. I am so awfully far away and can't possibly come until this strife is over. I pray for the sparing of Dad. All day my cry is for his life. Oh God will spare him till I return. And you my poor little Mother. Bear up for my sake and Charlie's. Please God this letter gets through ... Well darling bear up a little longer, the war can't go on much longer. Heaps of love to you all ...

The irony of Jack's deciding there and then to escape from Döberitz and return to Australia to be with his father is that Jack was unaware that his father had died of septic pneumonia three months prior to his receiving the letter telling him of his father's illness. In fact the letter informing him of his father's death never reached Jack and the news of his passing was only discovered weeks later, and in quite different circumstances.

Jack decides to escape

There is little doubt that Jack's decision to escape illustrates not only his courage and willingness to back himself against the odds, but also demonstrates something of the impulsiveness he had displayed on a number of previous occasions.

Within hours of making his decision Jack linked up with Geoffrey Whitlock, a fellow prisoner who had also been preparing to escape.

ALIVE TO TELL THE TALE.—IV.

ESCAPE FROM A GERMAN PRISON CAMP.

Mons Man Who Hid in a Ship's Locker.

BRAVE STRUGGLE FOR LIBERTY.

By G. H. WHITLOCK.

[Mr. Whitlock was a private, aged 18, in the 4th Middlesex Regiment (The "Die Hards") in August 1914. He went to France, was captured by the Germans at the Retreat from Mons and sent to a prisoners-of-war camp outside Berlin.

He made three attempts to escape, being successful the third time, after suffering many privations. Between his escape and his arrival in London he travelled 2,100 miles over land and sea. He was admitted to hospital suffering from frost-bite, and was awarded the Military Medal for his exploit.]

HIGH up on the hill above Doberitz, a suburb of Berlin, is a cemetery. Inside its gates is an imposing granite monument of a kneeling woman, weeping, her face buried in her hands. Pillars linked by chains encircle its base.

It is a memorial to the hundreds of allied soldiers who died in captivity in the prisoners-of-war camp that used to stand on the hill.

"Hungry Hill" Camp it was called in those far-off days of 1914. "Hungry Hill" it certainly was. When I enlisted in the Middlesex Regiment my record sheet showed my weight as 11st 4lb. When, four years later, I was discharged after two spells at "Hungry Hill," 7st 1lb were the figures.

I was sent to Doberitz following my capture at the British retreat from Mons. Changed conditions soon lowered my health. I fell a victim to dysentery. When I recovered I was sent out to work for the Corporation of Hohenschonhausen, another Berlin suburb.

Remuneration was equivalent to 2d a day. Our employers paid 8d a day to the German military authorities for our services. Pay was made in notes of a currency issued only to prisoners-of-war.

method by which they came ashore. They descended the ship's ladder and got into a small boat, which they pulled across to a number of barges.

Then they crossed the barges and so scrambled ashore.

Returning to the public-house, I had a drink, and made for the point where they had landed, firm in my determination to board the boat by the same means as they had left it. I decided to bluff the sentry if he stopped me.

It was snowing heavily as I crossed the barges, and as I swiftly paddled the small boat across to the ship I saw that the sentry was sheltering from the piercing wind and whirling flakes.

"Good-night," he called out, as, having climbed up the ship's ladder, I clambered aboard and walked along the deck. He had mistaken me for one of the crew.

In the Locker.

At once I made for the crew's quarters, which were deserted. I searched for a hiding-place, and presently found a trapdoor. I opened it and shone an electric torch into the dark cavity. It was a storeroom. I jumped down and landed on my feet.

Now I was alone excepting for an army

Excerpt from the article by Jack's fellow escapee, Geoffrey Whitlock, in the Sydney Morning Herald of 3 December 1938. It recounts his three escape bids, the first of which was with Jack; he was successful at the third attempt.

They had already talked frequently as they marched to and from the camp and worked together at various sites for the Corporation of Hohenschonhausen. They had not only devised plans, but had been working together to compile individual escape kits. Jack's desperation to see his father triggered his plans.

As part of their preparation both had put aside money for train fares and food. They were paid two pfennigs a day by the German military authorities, and they earned a further eight pfennigs from the Corporation of Hohenschonhausen. But their Corporation pay was made in POW notes, and without normal German currency their escape would be seriously handicapped. However a chance to save money in local currency came when they were both given the job of distributing flour and potatoes to local shopkeepers (on the production of ration cards). Whitlock later described how a nod, a wink and an extra kilogram or two slipped into the bag of the shopkeeper was quickly recognised as a 'tip', and the grateful burghers, short on rations but not money, were only too willing to compensate the two men for their carelessness! Three months of illicit transactions had brought them each between 1,200 and 1,300 marks, about £75 in English currency and sufficient, in their calculations, for an escape.

Forty-eight hours after deciding to make their break the two men managed to evade the guards as they returned to the camp after work. It was 6 September. The day before they had hidden suits of civilian clothes under straw in a nearby barn, and having slipped away from their gang undetected they quickly changed. Because they were both well known in Hohenschonhausen, they elected to bypass the town and make their way on foot via another suburb to catch a train to Berlin.

Once clear of their fellow prisoners they cut across several fields and through some woods to Weissensee. There, with characteristic bravado, they entered the small railway station and in fluent German Jack purchased tickets for the next train to Berlin. Whitlock relates that on reaching Berlin they were forced to stroll the city for several hours before again making their way to the main railway station, this time to catch the train to Stettin, a fortified seaport town on the North Sea near the mouth of the River Oder. Their idea, says

Jack's escape route to Malmö in September 1917.

Whitlock, was 'to catch the midnight train to that city and then try to board a neutral boat sailing to a neutral country'. They both spoke fluent German and again experienced no difficulty in obtaining their tickets.

The two men arrived at Stettin without incident early the following morning. Jack's seafaring knowledge and experience led them easily to the docks, and within a short time they struck up a conversation with a couple of friendly Swedish sailors waiting in the local hostelry for their ship to sail. Whitlock relates that it was not long before 'I told the truth about ourselves. They agreed to help us escape in their boat, the *Auraor** bound for [the neutral Swedish port of] Stockholm'.

When evening fell a couple of hours later the sailors took the two men amidships to a hatchway leading directly to the ship's bunker where they were to hide, at least until the ship's departure. Down the chute they slid into the pitch darkness of the hold. As the bunker was right next to the ship's boiler the heat was intense, but they were buoyed by the thought that they had made another substantial step towards freedom. They settled uneasily for the night on their hard bed of coal.

The morning brought unexpected problems. They were suddenly awoken by the noise of working cranes. This was followed by the tramp of feet overhead before the hatchway suddenly flew open, 'and half a ton of black coal poured down the chute in a thunderbolt of dust and noise'. They were very nearly buried. Dust and fumes filled their eyes, noses and throats, making them feel they would choke or suffocate. Worse still, they discovered that they had lost their precious bottles of water and the sandwiches they had brought with them.

They spent the next three days and nights in this uncomfortable hole, firmly wedged up to their chins in coal and without food or water. On the fourth day they heard the clang of bells. The engines throbbed, the boat shuddered, and the piled coal slipped ominously as the winch weighed anchor. They were about to get under way. Suddenly, however, the engines stopped, the anchor was dropped, and they heard voices – German voices, speaking urgently. The chute burst open, sending a stab of brilliant sunlight into the bunker and illuminating in its shaft the unfortunate Whitlock. After nearly 105 hours in the bunker he was once again a prisoner of the Germans.

Unbelievably, in the turmoil and noise that followed the capture of his colleague Jack somehow remained undetected. Whitlock gave no indication than he was not alone. Perhaps Jack's earlier experience working on board a windjammer carrying coal across the Pacific helped him to use the circumstances to best advantage. He simply

---

* The *Sydney Morning Herald* report gives the ship's name as *Auraor*, but this may well be a misprint for *Aurora*. We have been unable to confirm the ship's name.

buried himself deep in the coal as the Germans' attention was riveted on Whitlock, who was forced to clamber out of the bunker and into the hands of the triumphant German military police.

Jack survived without food or water for nearly another three days, before eventually crawling out of the *Auraor*'s bunker in Malmö, Sweden, a free man. His dash to freedom from Döberitz to Malmö that September in 1917 had taken him a total of eleven days. For his courage he was awarded the Military Cross.

CHAPTER 5

Flying Machines

Jack spent the first two weeks of his freedom recuperating in the sanctuary of the British Consulate, a spread of white buildings overlooking the harbour. His first task had been to cable his step-mother Elsie May with the news of his escape. In a return cable Jack learned of his father's death in a Melbourne hospital just a few days after having surgery for throat cancer.

Although profoundly grief-stricken, Jack found distractions from the sad news as he recuperated at the British Consulate. The story of his escape from Germany had spread quickly through the city, and Sweden being a neutral country, the audacity of his escape and his reason for doing so led to wide acclamation. In a small, informal ceremony just prior to his departure for England, Jack was presented to the King of Sweden at his Summer Palace in Malmö in public recognition of his escape.

At the end of September 1917 Jack returned to England through the Scottish port of Aberdeen and travelled south by train to London to take a few days of deserved leave, before deciding on his next move.

Changes

It must have been a most satisfying feeling to arrive safely back in London just on three years after he had first clambered aboard the SS *Cestrian* as a twenty-year-old Rifleman for the Western Front. But in those three years of captivity, the war had changed in ways that no one could have anticipated. Jack's first year as a prisoner had been one of sheer frustration for the Allies. The trench deadlock in France had resulted in little gain but huge numbers of casualties. Air raids had begun, and for the first time civilians found themselves innocent victims. Zeppelins brought destruction from the sky. Poison gas, a weapon that seemed to break all the chivalrous rules of war, had been introduced, first by the Germans but almost immediately adopted by the Allies. More significantly, the year had been marked by the growing acceptance of both sides that the original bright hopes for a swift return to peace were not to be easily or quickly realised.

The following year, 1916, had been one of sheer relentless killing. The Germans mounted a massive attack against the garrison city of Verdun in north-eastern France in a battle that not only claimed hundreds of thousands of lives, but in the process scarred the French psyche. For years after one could visit the sites of ghost villages uninhabited since the final days of this battle, but still religiously cherished as shrines to the massive losses experienced. The British suffered their own Verdun – on the Somme, where thousands of eager young volunteers died on the chalk downlands of Picardy, and where much of the original spirit of patriotic optimism that had inspired them to enlist dissolved in the mud.

The year in which Jack arrived back in England, 1917, was largely a year of pessimism and confusion, although as the year advanced it was not without hints of better things to come. Early blockades had threatened to fatally debilitate Britain. Widespread mutinies took place in the French army after the dismal failures of overly optimistic French initiatives. A little later, in July, the major push by the British – a three-and-half-month marathon now generally named after its final objective, Passchendale – had ground almost to a halt in the mud of the Third Ypres front, much as previous attempts had in the mud of the Somme. The mood in Britain was despondent, although it was not yet realised that the Germans were being debilitated even more seriously.

In early September, at the time Jack was making his way to Sweden, the Americans heralded their intention to enter the war on the Allied side. Later, immediately following his return to England, the French achieved a small but notable success under General Pétain on the Aisne; the Italians, despite severe pressure from the Germans, held their line on the River Pliave; and British tanks for the first time won a spectacular (if unexploited) success at Cambrai. Thus Jack's return to London was marked by glimmers of ultimate, if not immediate, hope for an Allied victory.

Tracking the changes

The Public Records Office (PRO) at Kew is a large and impressive building situated near the Thames River, London and boasting nearly 170 kilometres of shelving holding the records of hundreds of years of British history.

John had spent two days in a frustrating and unproductive search for information on Jack in the period between 1912 and 1919. Not a hint of Jack's name existed in either the Other Ranks' or the Officers' records. There was nothing in the POW records, and nothing in the medal records. Officials apologetically explained that many of the records from the Great War had suffered badly during the Battle of Britain in 1941. In fact, the PRO staff were still manfully rescuing many of the partially destroyed files, which after fifty years still remained to be restored and correctly filed. Sometime before the autumn of 2002 they were hoping to begin restoring the files under the letter P!

John decided to try the Royal Flying Corps files, hoping that Jack's files may have moved with his various changes in status. On the final afternoon he had set aside for the search John made one last check at the records counter. He was handed a dusty, brown cardboard box, at the bottom of which lay a manila folder containing about 25 flimsy, age-stained papers. He realised that he had at last found something special.

Back in the reading room a cursory scan revealed a trove of memoranda, letters and official notes. There amongst the pages was Jack's original application form to the Royal Flying Corps, as well as some letters in his own hand. The file included his final flying test results, together with his instructor's opinion on his last test fight before acquiring his wings. There was also a letter from his stepmother seeking his return to Australia.

It was an eerie feeling. John had discovered part of a man's personal history that had remained undisturbed for over 80 years.

Re-enlistment

One can only guess what might have gone through Jack's mind at the time of his return to England. He remained a Rifleman in the British Army, though the company he had originally joined in 1912, the Rifle Brigade, had been almost totally obliterated by the German offensives in the first months of fighting. The men who had survived were either German prisoners of war or had been reassigned in the early months of 1915 to companies in newly established British battalions. There was certainly little incentive for Jack to return to the incessant trench warfare that raged in France. He would have been confident that his three years of captivity in Döberitz, his escape, his likely award of a medal and possible promotion to officer rank would stand him in better stead in the continuing conflict, and release him from slogging it out in the trenches as an infantryman.

His attention turned to the Royal Flying Corps. His thinking was not unique. Charles Bean, the official Australian War Historian, gives a neat and insightful view of how so many young men like Jack, seeking relief from the trenches in France of 1916 and 1917, had begun to turn their eyes aloft. 'Trenches,' Bean says, 'simply wore out the hearts of men, so much so that wounds, and sometimes even death, came to be counted as blessings.' It is not hard to imagine that Jack saw the Flying Corps as an appealing alternative. Besides, the rapid establishment of new squadrons required a constant intake of young pilot cadets to feed the appetite of the escalating war in the air.

Therefore, on his return to London in late September, Jack applied for a transfer from the Rifle Brigade to the Flying Wing of the British Army, which together with the Royal Naval Wing was known as the Royal Flying Corps. On 5 October he passed his medical and seven days later, on 12 October, a month after crawling out of the coal bunker in Malmö, he was accepted into the Royal Flying Corps Officer Cadet Wing. He was ordered to report, on the expiration of his leave on 3 December 1917, to the No. 1 Cadet Wing of the Royal Flying Corps, located just south-west of London at St Leonards.

The Royal Flying Corps

When Jack enlisted in the RFC substantial changes had already taken place in the development of both aeroplanes and aerial tactics. At the beginning of the war the embryonic Corps used machines like Farmans and Caudrons, which took ten minutes to climb to a height of 1,000 metres, had a radius of action limited to 250 kilometres, and flew at a maximum speed of just 90 km/h. Aside from just being sent out 'to see what they could see' (an early form of reconnaissance), pilots would sometimes drop handfuls of *fléchettes* (small steel darts) at the enemy. The few squadrons that existed comprised three flights, each with four planes, and, if lucky, a couple of reserve machines.

By the early months of 1918, while Jack was completing his preliminary training, Scouts, for example, were flying at 250 km/h and climbing in five minutes to 3,000 metres. The RFC, which had become the Royal Air Force (RAF), had grown to a force of 300,000 men, and had 201 squadrons and 22,000 machines. By this time, aerial supremacy had begun gradually to shift away from the Germans as the Allies solved the problem of firing machine-guns through the propeller, and planes like the faster Sopwith Snipes and SE5As became increasingly available.

Initial training

With his medical out of the way, Jack was dispatched to St Leonards where he spent the following six weeks in preliminary training. His time was filled with lectures on the theory of flight and aerial navigation, as well as instruction in the design of aircraft and aero-plane engines. He gained practical experience with aero engines, in rigging, Morse code, elementary artillery observation, bombing and map reading.

Having successfully completed this stage, in early February 1918 he was sent for further instruction to the No. 1 School of Aeronautics at Reading, near London, where he entered an elementary training squadron. Here he began the more serious part of his initial training, where he was expected after three hours of dual instruction to complete at least an additional four hours solo. The squadron flew planes like Maurice Farmans and Graham Whites, but by the end of 1917

The young flyer. Jack photographed in May 1918 during initial training with the Royal Flying Corps.

new cadet pilots like Jack were beginning to use Avros. In his photograph album his training Avro makes frequent appearances – including photographs that record his first 'stack' later in the year.

Those who topped elementary training were generally selected for more intensive training in the Scout squadrons, which were equipped with new, fast and light machines. The other successful cadets were sent to fly various dual-seaters like Avros and Gnomes, used for ferrying tasks across the country. Jack was transferred to No. 56 Training Squadron where he completed 63 hours solo and 32 hours

Jack in a Sopwith Snipe, No. 6198, on 5 October 1918.

dual, including considerable cross-country flying. As a result he developed good navigational skills. This part of his training program also tested his reactions in emergency situations – he was required to climb to 2,500 metres, shut off his engine and land without engine assistance.

The training program also included night landings guided by flares, bomb-dropping, photographing points of given map reference, and shooting at targets on the ground from both the ground and the air. Pilots also had to learn to fly in formation, and to strip and assemble a Vickers or Lewis machine-gun!

On 5 November 1918 Jack won his 'wings' and graduated as a commissioned officer in the Royal Air Force.

A parallel agenda

The news of Jack's escape from Germany twelve months prior to his graduation as a Second Lieutenant in the RFC had begun an interrelated chain of events. With the loss of her husband in 1917, Jack's step-mother, knowing that he was now free, sought to bring her son home to Melbourne. She argued in letters and through representations to the military authorities by members of the family in England

Jack with unidentified plane, which appears to be an Avro 504K.

that, having been a prisoner for three years, some consideration was warranted for his return to Australia. The day following the arrival of the cable from Malmö she had written to the Commander of the Rifle Brigade in London requesting his support in bringing her son home to Australia. This was the beginning of a long and frustrating correspondence between her and the military authorities, the successful closure of which was brought about only by the timely end of the war itself.

In the few months following Jack's arrival in Malmö Elsie May lost all contact with her son, although every endeavour was made to locate him. The bureaucracy simply defeated her. Letters were returned stamped 'Unable to Trace' and her lack of success was compounded by Jack's transfer orders being mistakenly issued under someone else's name. With no response to her enquiries after six months, in a final desperate measure Elsie May enlisted the help of the Secretary of the YMCA in London. A letter from the secretary to the Rifle Brigade, enclosing a letter from his step-mother and asking Jack to consider returning home, eventually reached him in early February, just as he was leaving Reading for the second stage of his initial training at Hendon. Jack penned a letter to his Commanding

P.S.
The case from
Malmö was
dated 17th Sept 1917.

c/o Richardson Kerr Pty.Ltd
46. William Street
Melbourne
Victoria
Australia.
18th Sept. 1917.

The Commandant
The Rifle Brigade.

Dear Sir.

I am writing to you to let
you of the escape from Germany, of my Son
John. W. Probert. No. 4821. 1st Btn Rifle Brigade
I was advised by the British Consul at.
Malmoe, Sweden. that he was proceed-
ing to London. Now I am most anxious
for him to come home to Australia, as
I have lost. my husband (his father) and
am frightfully lonely. My son has been a
prisoner for three years. and I am sure
you will see all these sad circumstances.
I am writing to his Aunt. to ask her to
communicate with you. Her husband is
Colonel W.G. Probert. Hoping that you will
do all in your power. Yours faithfully
Elsie. M. Probert.

Elsie May's letter seeking the return of her stepson.

dated **4.11.18**   Headquarters
                     56th Wing,
                     Royal Air Force.

O.C., 41 T.D.S.,
    LONDON COLNEY.

    2nd.Lieut. J.W. Meule Probert.

     I have examined the above Flight Cadet and
find that he does not fly sufficiently well to make an
instructor. His turns are erratic as he does not make
the best use of the horizon, and his gliding turns re-
quire brushing up. He has already had over 30 hours
dual and the only way he will improve is with flying
practice. I beg to recommend that he be employed in
ferrying duties, and later, when he has done much more
flying, he may be found suitable as an instructor.

                                  A. Lanenfelder
                                     Captain.
               Wing Examining Officer.

"Whitehall"
CHINGFORD, Essex.
AF/ES.

*Jack's flying examination, which concluded that he would not make
an instructor.*

Officer seeking consideration for a transfer to the Australian Air Force
and requesting his return, once commissioned, to Australia on com-
passionate grounds.

    The correspondence in Jack's old RFC file leaves no doubt that
the British authorities were sympathetic to his request. They went as

An undated photograph of Jack in RFC uniform (Second Lieutenant), towards the end of the war.

far as suggesting that he seek to complete his training to a level of proficiency that would enable them to transfer him to the Australian Air Force as an instructor, so that he could train pilots in Australia.

Two factors intruded on this neat plan. Firstly, the Australian authorities had not been asked by the British whether they were prepared to accept Jack as pilot, let alone as an instructor. When they eventually were asked, they responded that they were unable to do so under the existing regulations. By way of concession, the Australians were prepared 'to press the case with [their] Headquarters in Australia to accept [Jack] as an instructor in Australia and to transfer him as a special case'.

Secondly – and more tellingly – Jack failed to gain the necessary 'A' grading at the end of his course, the minimum requirement to become an instructor. His instructor's report noted 'his turns were erratic, he did not make the best possible use of his horizon and his gliding turns required brushing up'. Nevertheless, the report left him with a glimmer of hope for the future when it suggested that after further flying experience there was every chance he could prove suitable as an instructor. For the time being his return to Australia was shelved.

No. 1 Fighting School,
Royal Air Force,
TURNBERRY, Ayrshire.
18th. December 1918.

Mrs. C. Moule-Probert,
The Pines,
Irving Ave.,
Armadale,
MELBOURNE....Australia.

```
NO. 1 FIGHTING
    SCHOOL
 18 DEC 1918
   IFS/97/1566
ROYAL AIR FORCE
```

Dear Madam,

I very much regret to have to confirm news which no doubt
you will have had by cable, that your son, 2/Lt. J.W. Moule-Probert,
was seriously injured in an aeroplane accident which took place at
the aerodrome here on Tuesday, 17-12-18 at about 11-30 a.m.

In the course of a flight his machine "stalled" and spun
to the ground, with the result that your son sustained serious
injuries, being badly hurt in the mouth, and nose and face in general.
He was admitted at once to the Reception Hospital here where he is
under the care of the Station Medical Officer, and making, so far, as
can be said now, satisfactory progress.

Under the regulations of the Royal Air Force we are not
allowed to cable abroad to the relatives of Officers or other ranks
injured in the course of their duty and this explains why I have not
sent a cable to you, but as the accident was immediately reported to
the Air Ministry by telegram I have no doubt that you have been informed by this time, and I mention this matter so that you will understand
that it is not a lack of courtesy which has caused me not to cable
direct to you, but the regulations of the Air Force.

By the time this letter reaches you I suppose this information will not be correct to date, but I will write you again in
the course of a few days to confirm the condition of your son as he
is then.   You may rest quite assured that he will receive the
best of medical attention, and everything possible will be done for
him.

I beg to remain,

Yours very faithfully,

Major, Asst. Commandant,
No. 1 Fighting School,
Royal Air Force.

RO/JM

The letter reporting Jack's second accident to his mother.

ROYAL AIR FORCE.   F.S. Form 558.

CASUALTY CARD.

Surname   **PROBERT**   2Lt.   Branch File No._____

Christian Name   *John William Moule*

Regiment   *R.A.F.*   Squadron *1 Fighting Sch Turnberry*

Date of Report.	By whom reported.	Reference to List.	Date of Casualty.	NATURE OF CASUALTY.	Date published in Press.
18/12/18	Turnberry	P3/2531 X200/3	17/12/18	*Injured serious (Aero acc) Ad Reception Hosp Turnberry*	

Jack's casualty card from his second crash at Turnberry. Note that the RFC was by now the Royal Air Force.

Not a whimper but two bangs

Jack's time in the RAF was both short and eventful. On 'winning his wings' he was transferred to No. 41 Squadron, but within days of his arrival peace was declared in Europe. In a personal and more than likely unauthorised marking of the event, he decided to celebrate Armistice Day just half an hour after its official declaration. His records note that he crashed his SE5A while performing 'celebratory aerobatics' of a type unlikely to be ever successfully achieved by such an aircraft. The crash probably dented his reputation more than the plane. However, two photographs in his album are dashingly captioned 'SE5A before and after contact with terra firma!'

The second 'stack' just a month later was far more serious. On 1 December Jack joined the No. 1 Fighter School of the RAF at Turnberry in Scotland. A letter from his commanding officer to his mother, dated 18 December 1918 (*shown opposite*) explained that

your son Second Lieutenant J.W. Moule-Probert was seriously injured in an aeroplane accident which took place at the aerodrome here on Tuesday 17 December 1918 at about 11.30 am.

In the course of a flight his machine 'stalled' and spun to the ground, with the result that your son sustained serious injuries, being badly hurt in the mouth, and nose and face in general.

Jack (left) returned to Australia on the SS Heluan.
Here he plays deck quoits, still dressed in uniform.

Jack remained in hospital for five weeks to recover from surgery, which involved the insertion of a silver metal plate into his skull. This drastic treatment was needed to help knit the severe head fracture he had sustained in the crash. A further three months of recuperation followed in London, and in May 1919 he was declared sufficiently fit to be finally repatriated to Australia.

CHAPTER 6

Back in Civvies –
a Farmer's Life

Jack spent the greater part of the years between the wars as a farmer. In this respect he was not unlike thousands of other returned men who in the early 1920s took up the Australian Government's offer of land and became soldier settlers.

As we reconstructed the story of this period two sources proved immensely helpful. The first was an old cash and wage book, purchased to keep track of the family's budget. Jack used it as a farm journal somewhat irregularly over a period of seven years, but it contained enough information to help us to fill in the bleak detail of the family's battle to survive the hardships of this period. As we pored over the minutiae of farm life – the records of sales of wheat and oats, income from the occasional sale of turkeys, the numbers of ewes and lambs that died from toxemia, monies owed to Dalgetys*, rainfall records, numbers of fence posts cut and sold to local farmers, the agistment arrangements for their horses – the struggle that it all represented emerged from its pages.

Our other source was the revealing stories written by sons and daughters of the early settlers of the Rankins Springs district, published as a book, *Conapaira Links,* by the local historical society in 1998. These stories of the early days of the district not only triggered our own long-dormant memories, but revealed a tapestry of insights into everyday life that tellingly conveyed the spirit and determination of soldier settlers like Jack.

---

* A large wool broking and rural finance firm founded in 1884 by F.G. Dalgety and popularly known as 'Dalgetys'.

Finally, in an attempt to recapture the sights and sounds of a farm that represented over fourteen years of Jack's life, we returned one late autumn afternoon a couple of years ago and simply sat on the hill looking northwards over the farm. It was an uncanny experience.

The 'between years'

When Jack when returned home in June 1919, not only had he changed markedly, but he found this world far different from the one he had left as a youth nine years previously. He was now just one of the many thousands of young men who, after their overseas war experiences, were full of enthusiasm and vigour to make a better life for themselves.

Young Australians like Jack had never experienced the Old World in such numbers or for so long, at such an impressionable age, and they came back with a renewed confidence in being Australian. Many claim they returned with a new pride in the battle-tried prowess of the Australian fighting man, and with a greater appreciation of the material living standards and the roomier, sunnier life that Australia offered. Their changed views influenced the new generation and began to engender a sense of identity that was distinctly Australian, and less 'British'.

There was no doubt that the Great War had touched almost every family in the country one way or another. Australia's population had barely reached 5 million in 1918, yet during the war Australia managed to raise almost 417,000 volunteer troops. Half of these were less than 25 years old when they joined up, and of these many were less than 20. The numbers represented almost 10 per cent of the Australian population, and, significantly, almost half its youth. Of those that enlisted 330,000 went overseas, and almost 70 per cent of these – the highest proportion of any Empire country – were casualties of one kind or another: 60,000 died, about 160,000 were wounded and nearly 60,000 fell ill in the dreadful conditions encountered on the battlefields. The huge numbers of dead and wounded brought worry, hardship and years of silent grief into thousands of Australian homes; yet this sense of suffering became a significant force in working considerable changes in the Australian way of life.

The returned Australian soldiers formed a distinctive group in most Australian communities and their elite status was confirmed each Anzac Day. Many ex-servicemen seemed deliberately to set themselves apart from other Australians, yet at the same time they devoted great energy to helping their wounded comrades and bereaved families. The Returned Services League gradually emerged as a conservative social organisation and a significant influence in helping returned men to ease their way back into civilian life.

It was also a time when a broad current of idealism was beginning to run through much of the Australian community. There was a growing determination to build, in the rather ponderous words of some of the politicians of the day, a land 'fit for heroes'. 'Our boys must have the best' claimed a popular slogan of the time. For a large number of these returned 'boys', the best was a block of land to be turned into a farm.

In the years immediately following the war nearly 37,000 men settled on the land under the Soldier Settlement Scheme, unwittingly subscribing to the fatal myth that land could be worked cheaply and would provide an adequate livelihood. The state bodies administering the scheme were overwhelmed by applications from huge numbers of enthusiastic returned men, the majority of whom had little or no farm experience or capital, but who possessed an unlimited abundance of energy. Unfortunately, because of the overwhelming demand most state authorities were forced to reach into marginal farming country to secure sufficient land for those they accepted. As a result the returned soldiers spilt out onto the edges of the wheat belt of Western Australia, the northern mallee in Victoria and the plains of the central Riverina. They moved to newly established irrigation areas of the Riverland along the Murray, the steep hills of the dairy belts of New South Wales, and to the edges of the inland tropics in Queensland.

The fortunate soldiers won blocks subdivided from sheep and cattle stations in the more hospitable parts of the country. However, the speed with which the scheme moved, swept along by a wave of patriotic fervour, proved disastrous for a large number of the new settlers. There was too little training, too little capital for investment,

Photos from Jack's album.

Living it up at Portsea, Victoria, 1920. Jack is standing.

Jack captioned this photo 'Some of the wags at Lorne'. Lorne in 1921 was a popular Victorian beach resort. Jack, in the front, is obviously very much one of the 'wags'.

Another of Jack's album snaps, captioned 'School's in'. Jack is at front left.

too little investigation of the soil and climate, and, ultimately, too many under-sized blocks.

By 1929, as the world recession ate into the prices of most primary products, around two-thirds of the original settlers remained on their farms. A decade later, as Australia began to lift itself out of its own Depression, over a half of the original soldier settlers had disappeared from the land.

After the war

We know little about Jack in the years immediately following the war, apart from vague family recollections and oblique references drawn from stories recalled years afterwards by people who knew him. Our sketchy knowledge of the three or four years immediately after his return is supplemented by a few old Box Brownie photos from family albums, but they provide fleeting and incomplete glimpses of his life at this time.

At this particular time Australia was marked by high unemployment (around 12 per cent in the early 1920s), and while preference was given to returned servicemen work was not always easy to come by even for them. The small gratuity offered to returned servicemen by the Australian Government, his deferred pay and a small war pension would have greatly assisted Jack's day-to-day living. During this period he may have completed various stints of farm labouring and share farming around Victoria, at places like Kerang. There is a strong likelihood that he worked with friends made during the war who had returned to work on the land. Certainly a number of his photos suggest this.

As a man in his mid-twenties, with almost a lifetime's worth of experience already squeezed into the years behind him, he almost certainly believed that life was now to be enjoyed to the full. There are snapshots in his albums of summer beach parties and holidays spent in fashionable summer beach resorts, like Lorne and Portsea near Melbourne.

Jack probably recommenced flying at this time. As H.C. Miller, the founder of McRobertson Miller Airlines in Western Australia, points out in his autobiography *The Early Birds*, for many of the men who had experienced it during the war flying became a highly personal and almost an all-consuming force. Here was an occupation that promised not only excitement but also new opportunities. Paradoxically, while it might have been a perilous job during the war, it was now a relatively secure job for the war veteran. Mention has been made of Jack flying as a courier between Sydney and Melbourne. Just how accurate these stories are is impossible to verify, yet they seem to fit the nature of the man and certainly the sense of the times.

Becoming a farmer

As a result of the introduction of the Soldier Settlement Scheme Jack won a Farmstead Lease of 1,555 acres (630 hectares) in mallee country 13 kilometres south of the small township of Rankins Springs in the western plains of New South Wales. It was virgin country, but at the time the acreage was regarded as large enough to establish a successful, self-sufficient, dry area wheat farm. Jack also received an advance of £1,000 from the Commonwealth government to cover some of the initial costs involved in clearing, fencing and establishing a water supply on his new farm. The advance was also to help offset costs such as purchasing implements, stock and seed, and building materials.

An annual rent of 2.5 per cent of the value of the farm was levied, with repayments spread over 38 years, although a moratorium was given for the first two repayments. Jack's first annual repayment in December 1926 was £2/2/8. In lieu of paying an annual rental in each of the next five years, he was also given the option to spend the equivalent sum on farm improvements, provided he obtained prior permission from the Office of the Lands Commission. Jack expected that when all necessary conditions had been met he would have a lease in perpetuity over his own farm; for all practical purposes, the equivalent of freehold title over what he hoped would provide his future.

On 24 July 1924, the farm he called 'Womalilla' was gazetted, with Jack Probert as its first landholder.

Set up to fail

In hindsight, examining the early years of the Soldier Settler Scheme makes it painfully obvious that the Scheme was doomed to fail. The speed with which it was implemented proved disastrous for many. Most of the farmers had little or no capital to invest, despite having received initial financial support from the Scheme to offset early expenses. Too little investigation of soil and climate had been undertaken, and too many of the blocks were undersized and in very marginal farming country. Few men had the necessary training and experience in what for many was an alien occupation. On top of this it became quickly apparent that many of the administrators of the scheme, despite their enthusiasm, were clearly incompetent, and well out of their depth.

The difficulties faced by some ex-servicemen are illustrated in the personal diary of the wife of an early settler, who described in very colourful language how the government had established the two of them on a small three-hectare farm in Yanco, south-west New South Wales, and provided experts to advise them how to establish their peach orchard – only to find that when the trees matured a few years later no provision had been made to cater for the unexpectedly vast amount of fruit produced. Nor had officials made any provision for the fruit's processing. The farmers instead received £1 for each peach tree they destroyed, and they were forced to dig in the remaining peaches. The scenario was then repeated, this time with tomatoes. Insult was added to injury when, although the tomatoes were accepted for canning, this proved pointless because the canning service was inadequate. Most of the cans either bulged or exploded!

Some more fortunate settlers won potentially viable blocks when, for example, subdivisions were made of sheep and pastoral stations in the more hospitable parts of the country or in newly established irrigation areas. However, far too many were short-changed. They were left to clear dense bush from poor, marginally fertile land at a time when they had insufficient capital or know-how to achieve anything more than scraping an existence from the soil and compounding their debt.

The situation was exacerbated by external factors beyond anyone's control. Newcomers faced increasingly dry times, which deteriorated at times to extended drought. The late 1920s were also a time of unstable and generally falling prices for primary produce world-wide.

So, many of these returned men who had seen a soldier settler's block as a means to escape wage slavery and become masters of their own life were prematurely forced to face a rude disillusionment.

The district of Rankins Springs

The country surrounding Jack's new farm was, at best, only marginal farming land, and had only a very brief white history before he arrived. Apart from the Aboriginal tribes that moved across the country the first man to visit the Rankins Springs area was the explorer, John Oxley. During his explorations in 1817 he had travelled along the western edge of the Cocoparra Range and passed within a few kilometres of the site that was to become the town of Rankins Springs. He bluntly described the country as barren and desolate, and expressed doubt as to whether civilised man would ever pass that way again.

Nevertheless in 1858, a little over forty years later, Conapaira Station was given a lease of some 48,000 acres (19,500 hectares) near the future town. This became one of a number of large leases subsequently granted to pastoralists across the district who in the middle years of the last century squatted in these arid western expanses of scrubby land to run sheep. The NSW government had originally planned for an orderly, systematic and regulated colonisation of the west, but the pastoralists moved far too quickly into the empty country beyond the set limits, and simply squatted! With time the 'squattocracy' became respectable, leases were formally granted, and large pastoral tracts like those in the vicinity of Rankins Springs were gradually opened up through the latter years of the nineteenth century.

The origin of the name Rankins Springs is not definitely known, but it first appears in official records just prior to 1870. 'Rankin' as a place name is not uncommon and can be found in widely scattered parts of Australia. However, it seems likely that in this particular case the name came from the Rankin family, who arrived from Tumut to take up Ballandry Station in 1863 and found a valuable natural spring. Later a small town slowly grew up on the site, encouraged by the confluence of two important stock routes, Whitton to Lake Cargelligo and Woolongough to Hillston, the former running down the eastern boundary of what was to become Jack Probert's wheat farm.

Around the turn of the century and almost up to the time that Jack arrived on the block these roads echoed with the noise of Cobb and Co. mail and passenger coaches. Coach routes in this part of western NSW spread very rapidly. As the Victorian goldmines began to run down, Cobb and Co. looked to extend their coach lines. They moved swiftly to either absorb many of the then operating coach businesses in NSW, or, in current terminology, to franchise the more resistant ones. They created a huge network of routes linking the mining, pastoral and farming settlements with the various railheads being established throughout the region.

In the period leading up to the First World War these coaches conveyed a fascinating array of people: miners, government officials, station hands, commercial travellers, 'snaggers' who kept the rivers navigable, woodcutters who cut the fuel for the river steamers. And, crucial to the survival of the coach-line as well as the people of the area, the mail.

When Jack arrived in Rankins Springs in 1924 the great coach age was beginning to pass. Cars and coaches began to overlap. Motor cars and trucks were beginning to challenge the bullock wagon and the coach. Following a survey and a government undertaking to build railway line from Barmedman to Hillston by way of Rankins Springs, a hotel was built in 1892 to take advantage of the anticipated growth of the township. In 1915 the line was commenced, but because of the war its completion was delayed until early 1923. At this time parts of some of the large station properties surrounding Rankins Springs were resumed by the state authorities, cut up into smaller blocks and offered by ballot to the returned soldiers seeking dry area farms. In July 1924, Jack arrived to take up his new block.

The rough, one-room hut that Jack built shortly after taking up his soldier settlement block near Rankins Springs in 1924.

Early years on the farm

Jack faced a daunting task when he arrived, alone, at his newly-won block after a dusty, three-day drive from Sydney. There were no fences, no house and no permanent water. The country was largely untouched. The soil was red and porous, and scrubby stands of mallee and native pine covered the country. Access to his new farm was at a place of his own choosing, somewhere along the sandy Whitton to Lake Cargelligo stock route that skirted the eastern boundary.

The first few months of work may well have been the hardest he ever experienced. The first requirement was for shelter. On a clear elevated spot, flanked at the rear by mallee scrub and kurrajong, he built a rough, temporary one-room shack with pine slats, a flat corrugated galvanised iron roof and an earth floor. There were no windows, and hessian bags were used to cover the entrance. Water for drinking and washing came from a forty-four-gallon (200-litre) petrol drum just outside the entrance. A small, outdoor wood oven fuelled by mallee roots was set up close by.

The log cabin Jack built in 1925 for his wife, Minnie. The little girl is a neighbour's daughter, and the dog is Jack's dog 'Nick'.

His first year on the farm in 1924 has been described by the old timers of the district as 'a really good year'; rainfall exceeded 600 mm and the country looked wonderful. This undoubtedly encouraged Jack. He cleared land around the shack, built poultry yards, and commenced a more substantial house.

In the middle of 1925 Jack took some time off for a break in Sydney. Nobody knows whether he intended to stay for as long as he did, but early in his stay he met a 26-year-old English girl. After a whirlwind romance of three weeks, they were married in St Nicholas's Church of England in Brook Street, Coogee, on 8 June 1925. His new wife, Minnie, returned with him to 'Womalilla' after a further few weeks in Sydney, and for the next two-and-a-half years the two of them worked hard to establish the farm.

One of the first tasks was to complete the house. Jack had already cleared a spot close to the original shack, felled timber and begun the foundations. On the couple's return from Sydney he quickly finished the simple wooden home, which was roofed with galvanised iron, had split pine floorboards, and a lean-to at the back.

105

The 'tank' at Womalilla.

A second, equally important task faced them – a permanent water supply. Until this time Jack had relied on the vagaries of the rains, supplemented by water carried by Furphy cart from the railhead at Rankins Springs. He excavated a 'tank'* close to the north-eastern boundary of the farm. At the time most farmers were forced to build dams by hand, using shovels and picks, and, where possible, hired help. However, Jack was able to use a narrow, shallow scoop drawn by a couple of horses to drastically reduce the weeks of back-breaking digging ordinarily needed to prepare such a dam and its carefully graduated run-offs. 1926 was again a year of good rains, and the dam filled quickly.

Perimeter fences were a priority, so posts and strainers were cut as the land was cleared of its mallee trees. (It was a contractual stipulation that soldier settlers had to erect fences on all boundaries of

---

* A dam on a property was known locally as a 'tank'. A Furphy cart was a water cart made of cast iron by Victorian manufacturer J[ohn] Furphy & Son, Shepparton. (During World War 1 the carts had become centres of gossip, giving rise to the coinage 'furphy' for a false rumour.)

Mallee rolling with a team of horses.

their new block within five years of taking up their farm, or risk forfeiture.)

The government subsidised the purchase of wire netting for the fencing of these blocks. Entrepreneurial farmers who shared a common boundary often found themselves with just enough subsidised netting left over to construct a tennis court. There seems to have been no shortage of social tennis outings for a very large number of farmers!

As new settlers, similarly isolated and challenged by their circumstances, grew to know each other, typical country willingness to share ideas, labour and machinery emerged. The levelling and clearing of scrub for wheat was probably one of the more daunting challenges that had to be faced. Clearing the land using huge, single-bar log rollers, made from large, straight eucalypts and drawn by a team of horses, became a shared task. A number of photos in Jack's album show how he accomplished the massive task of clearing the dense mallee bush from his farm.

It was arduous and back-breaking work. Once the mallee had been felled and left to dry for a few months it was fired. This involved walking around the 'rolled' timber with a 'fire bucket' made from an old kerosene tin punctured with holes and with the top cut out.

Pulled along on its side with a wire handle, the hot coals were tipped out onto the combustible material. When the wind blew up unexpectedly it was not unknown for bushfires to catch in nearby stands of mallee. The smaller of the remaining stumps were removed by disc plough and carted away over the years; the bigger and more resistant ones were simply left, and crops planted around them.

For Jack and the other farmers who pioneered the Rankins Springs district the price was high. Huge distances, difficult, uncertain conditions, and demanding work made for financial and personal problems. During these years wheat provided at best a meagre living, and when the seasons were dry and crop yields dropped below subsistence levels it became a genuine struggle.

Real hardship began for most of the farmers in the district in 1927. The season was so dry that in desperation some 'sowed dry' in the hope that rains would come. No rain arrived, and as a result almost nothing germinated; where it did scavenging rabbits ensured nothing remained to be harvested. The year 1928 was kinder, allowing farmers to claw back a little and keep their heads above water. But worse was to come.

In these early years Jack's farm failed to provide enough income to meet the annual rental repayments, let alone buy the much-needed equipment to make farming viable. It was the meagrest of livings. Then, just two days before Christmas in 1927, his wife Minnie suddenly left, taking their two-year-old son John with her. The little that is known of the reasons for their separation and ultimate divorce suggests that a marriage that started with high hopes was undermined by the loneliness of living on a struggling farm, and the primitive and demanding living conditions. Minnie returned to Sydney, and Jack had no further contact with her or the child.

Tough times

The turn of the decade continued to bring tough times for Jack, now alone on the farm. Both 1929 and 1930 were dry and difficult years. The farm provided barely enough to allow him to continue. Nevertheless, in response to Government requests to wheat farmers to expand their acreage to offset falling wheat prices, he rolled many

Jack seated on the running board of a Hupmobile on his farm, early 1930s.

hectares of mallee in 1929. But while more wheat was grown, the world wheat price fell from six shillings a bushel in 1929 to less than three shillings in 1930, leaving farmers like Jack struggling to survive. In papers Jack filed for his divorce from Minnie the recognition of his failure as a wheat farmer is starkly evident. He admits that he was unable to grow wheat of a saleable quality, and could not make any profit. He had reached a point where he was almost prepared to relinquish the farm. But like so many others, he decided to stay on in the hope that both seasons and prices would improve.

In the midst of all this came the Great Depression. It is important to understand that for struggling farmers like Jack Probert – as indeed for most workers of the time – it became essential to stay in some kind of work. The alternative, extended unemployment, was soul-destroying. This was a time when not only were more people unemployed than at any other time in Australia's history, but they were unemployed for far longer periods. Unemployment in the Australian wage-earning class in 1933 was nearly 27 per cent. In the trough of this period the basic wage for a family of four was just over £3 a week, and government aid for those unemployed was seven shillings for a single man and 14 shillings for a married couple. The bleakness of the time can be recognised in the fact that in the middle of 1933 12 per cent of the population earned nothing at all; a quarter earned less than £1 a week; another 17 per cent earned less that £2 a week. This means that 54 per cent of families were earning less than two-thirds of the current basic wage. Was it any wonder that Australian society was beginning to change as the Depression tore through its old ways of living?

1931 brought minor relief for the farmers in the district, with heavy rains and good crops, but as it turned out this was their last reasonably productive year for the next seven. During this time most of the farmers were financially crippled, and large numbers simply walked off their farms empty-handed. Others who had become heavily indebted to private firms were declared bankrupt and their goods put up for auction. For a very fortunate few, in what was seen as a way of demonstrating good old Australian 'mateship' neighbours turned out in support and bought up as many of the auctioned goods as they could at the ridiculously low prices, then gave them back to their owners to help them continue on their farm. Those who stayed on faced tough and unyielding times, and it was clear that the district was now in a slow, inexorable decline.

Distractions from the farm
Some time around 1930 Jack Probert met Hugh Peach, a young twenty-year-old who had come from Sydney to work at the newly established Mirrool Packing Company in Griffith. The town was a growing centre for this new irrigation and fruit-growing area, and despite being in the midst of the Depression the district was attracting increasing numbers of people who saw the promise of work in difficult times. The township was also drawing many of the farmers from the outlying dry area farms, not only for shopping, but also for medical, hospital and similar professional services not available in the smaller centres. Jack Probert regularly drove his car the fifty-odd kilometres to Griffith to shop, purchase materials for the farm and meet friends. (When the weather was fine and warm he would sometimes

Jack in 'Big Bertha'.

hitch the horse to the sulky and make his way along the sandy stock route for the forty-odd kilometre trip to Yenda instead.) Perhaps his interest in flying was rekindled by seeing the Lakeview Aerodrome just on the outskirts of Griffith.

In the middle of that year Jack took a break from the farm and travelled the 650 kilometres to visit his new friend Hugh and his family in Harbord, on the northern beaches of Sydney. Here he met Hugh's older sister Nora, and though we can only speculate that he was immediately attracted to her, he invited her, her mother and brother Harold to visit his farm for a holiday later that year. Photos in his album reveal the story of a long, dusty, three-day trip for the Peaches in their 1927 'hard-top' Morris, first to Canberra and then through Beckom to Rankins Springs. They also show the family seeing for the first time the broad acres of ripening wheat, and their visits in Jack's soft-top tourer – nick-named 'Big Bertha' – to Griffith and Yenda. Jack and Nora probably decided to marry around this time, but it seems that Nora's mother had not been overwhelmingly impressed with either the house that Jack was living in or the struggle that he was experiencing with the farm. There appears to have been an agreement for the marriage to be delayed until such time as a reasonable house was built, prospects on the farm had improved and Jack's divorce from Minnie had been finalised.

According to a family story, Jack gave Nora an engagement ring that had been made from gold taken by his grandfather, William, from the goldfields of Bendigo. It reportedly had the family seal in black onyx set into it.

It was in the early period of Jack's and Nora's courtship that Hugh Peach almost lost his life in a flying incident in Griffith. At the time Jack had been doing a fair bit of flying, some of it in a relatively new Metal Moth registered VH-UNN. When it was brought new to Australia in May 1930 this plane was the 318th to be registered in the country. It was called a Metal Moth to distinguish it from a Gipsy Moth – it had a welded steel fuselage rather than the wooden one of the Gipsy, making it more sturdy. It was 7 metres long, had a wing span of 3 metres, and cruised comfortably at around 135 kilometres per hour.

Late at the end of a summer afternoon in January 1931, Hugh was a passenger in this same plane when it crashed on the Lakeview Aerodrome. For a number of days Hugh was in a critical condition in the local Woodlands Private Hospital. He took several weeks to recover, and then decided it was time to return to Sydney and seek new pastures.

Throughout this difficult period Jack Probert seems to have maintained his interest in flying, although his capacity to remain airborne was at times challenged. Jack Hall, an old Griffith identity, recalled Jack enlisting his services as a re-sleever on one occasion to machine the shaft and straighten the propeller of a plane after a minor bingle. Jack took him up for a flight as part payment, but the plane 'vibrated so much' and 'the velocity of the wind' was so great that when he landed again on the Dog Ground just south of the Main Canal he was grateful to have returned in one piece! Hall also described another occasion when Jack had been flying a small biplane early one morning and, as a result of a sudden wind gust, had collided with a large pine tree while attempting to land, pancaking somewhat unceremoniously onto the ground close to the Dog Ground. When the locals discovered the plane shortly afterwards there was no sign of the pilot, so they set out to look for him. They found him sitting nonchalantly in the Wallace Cafe having a large plate of eggs and bacon for

This page from Jack's album shows that he still felt the appeal of aviation. His caption reads 'Farmer and aviator? 1930'.

The plane crash that nearly claimed Hugh Peach's life. Jack had flown the Metal Moth VH-UNN at various times – it appears in his photo album (see page 113).

breakfast. As Hall commented, he was 'pretty cool – it took a lot to stir him up!'

Hall also remembers Jack Probert giving joy flights in a small biplane, and at one time flying what is assumed to be a DH83, which Hall recollects was used at the time as an ambulance plane. It had enclosed accommodation for four passengers – the pilot sat in a separate, open cockpit – and was much roomier and more economical than other planes of the period. This type of plane was used at the time by the Flying Doctor Service, and by the fledgling airline Qantas for its short domestic feeder services which were beginning to spread through Queensland and New South Wales.

Final years on the farm

Because it was becoming increasingly difficult to make a living from wheat growing, Jack, like many other farmers, decided that he needed to diversify. So in the latter part of 1931 he turned his attention to sheep. For an outlay of £21 he purchased from his neighbour Alan Cruickshank 22 ewes and a ram in order to begin a flock. At the same time he cut back substantially on the amount of wheat he sowed, and began to divide and fence the farm into a number of smaller 120

The log house for Nora takes shape.

hectare paddocks to accommodate the change in direction. At this stage little mallee remained on the farm – just a few stretches along the northern and southern boundary fences and a few isolated stands in parts of the west paddock. One paddock was left fallow and another for sowing wheat.

In 1932, although he only received £6/19/– for his wool cheque, when it was added to his wheat bounty there seemed to be a glimmer of hope that things would change for the better. He felt encouraged to continue.

In early 1933, in anticipation of his marriage, Jack built a new pine-log house cut from trees on the block, near the site of the previous shack. In June, he married Nora Peach in St Albans Church in Griffith. His new wife was 26, almost 12 years younger than Jack. She had, coincidentally, been born in the cathedral town of St Albans in England, and had arrived with her family in Australia in 1911 when only six. The family had settled in Harbord, a northern beach suburb of Sydney, and she had completed her education at Fort Street Girls High School, one of the foremost public schools in New South Wales. She was a gentle, well-read girl, who wrote poetry and had worked as a book-keeper at the National Cash Register Company in the city in the years following her secondary schooling.

This new life on a dry area farm in outback New South Wales must have been daunting for a city girl. Amenities were rudimentary. Water for washing and bathing was at a premium and had to be brought by a Furphy cart from the dam and kept in drums outside the house. Alum or Epsom salts were added regularly to the drums to clear the water, and bath water was diligently used to maintain the garden plants that surrounded the house.

Apart from the small flock, a few sheep were kept as 'killers' for mutton. Meat was salted or made into a pickled brawn. Rabbits provided another source of meat, but were of limited appeal to Jack who had eaten numerous rabbits during his early years on the block. A cow provided milk, and the cream was occasionally turned into butter. Fowls provided eggs, and spare eggs were preserved in 'water-glass' (sodium silicate) in a kerosene tin for cooking at times when the fowls were not laying.

Food and drink were kept cool in a 'drip safe', which had a tray of water on top to keep the safe's hessian sides damp. A wood stove was used for cooking and kerosene lamps provided light at night. The walls inside the house were lined with hessian and furniture was sparse. To heat the house during winter a fire was lit outside in a kerosene tin with holes pierced in its sides – when the flames had died down to red-hot embers the tin was brought inside. A phone line had come from Griffith to Rankins Springs in the early 1930s but it operated only as a party line, with Morse code rings, when the local exchange happened to be manned.

As the seasons grew steadily drier, dust storms became frequent. Huge suffocating clouds of red dust from the Hay plains to the west would roll in, leaving layers of fine dust over everything. These storms were sometimes so severe that people were forced to place dampened cloths over their face to breathe.

While friends and family members from Sydney who came to stay would more often than not travel by car, the rail link to Rankins Springs provided a challenging alternative. A steam train consisting of dog boxes and bench seats left from Sydney's Central Station at 8 pm. At midnight there was a break at Goulburn for the train to take on water, and for a quick, cold dash by those awake to the refreshment room for steaming tea in heavy railway china cups. This was followed by a change of trains at Temora at breakfast time, then on to Barmedman for a final change. A stop was made at Weethallee for lunch, with enough time for a quick visit to the pub over the road or a sandwich from the corrugated iron cafe next door. The final stage was usually a mind-numbingly slow trip, with the train stopping at each and every small station to drop off passengers and mail, before eventually reaching Rankins Springs almost 24 hours after its Sydney departure.

Living on a farm was not always isolating. There were various social activities. Neighbours from surrounding farms had frequent 'get-togethers' at each other's houses to talk and play cards. There were dances around the district, with button accordions and violins, as well as regular tennis days. And of course there were the regular, all-day trips to Griffith or Yenda to shop, catch up with friends and sell farm produce.

By 1933 Jack had doubled the size of his sheep flock, and was receiving between fourpence-halfpenny and sevenpence-halfpenny a pound for the small amount of wool he shore. He stood a number of his mares to stallions belonging to neighbours, and introduced a few pigs which he was able to sell for 12/6 each at the sales in Griffith later in the year. From the outset Nora began to raise turkeys as a sideline. She sold these to the local Rankins Springs Hotel, or in Griffith to places like Mirrool House, the Mona Cafe and the Victoria Hotel (at sevenpence a dressed pound).

Farm scenes: Jack on the way to market with bales of wool; Jack stooking hay; Jack's future brother-in-law, Hugh Peach, in a wheat field with Nora and her mother, Leah.

The following year, 1934, was mixed. They harvested a disappointing total of 22 bags of wheat, 16 bags of oats and 5 tonnes of hay. The flock, which now comprised comebacks (a cross between a Border Leicester ram and a merino ewe, prized for its wool quality) and crossbreds, slowly built to a hundred, but even with the sale of a few ewes at 3/7 each and the wool clip bringing in sixpence a pound it was still a struggle. Nora found that through judicious husbandry she was able to increase her flock of turkeys to almost a hundred, despite crows making frequent inroads into the pullets. To supplement their income they sold poles to local contractors, agisted sheep and cattle for neighbours, hired horses to one of the local mills for 10/- a week, leased access to their dam to a contractor for £1 a week (who in turn carried water and sold it to local people), sold sheep skins to Dalgetys for between 1/6 and 4/6, depending on the weight of wool, and disposed of lambs at the grand price of around 12/6. At one stage during the year, Jack even worked for a short time at Campbell's timber mill in Rankins Springs at 15/- a day. (It was not unusual at the time for farmers to hold down a second job.) After all this, Jack's farm journal reveals that their net return was a meagre £56 for the year.

The years from 1932 to 1939 represented a long and difficult drought for the Rankins Springs district, with only 1936 providing any break to the pattern. Farmers struggled, and their poor returns generally prevented them from making any real reduction to the debts on their farms. The Commonwealth Government had recognised as far back as 1930 the predicament facing many of the soldier settlers, and established the Rural Reconstruction Board with the express purpose of consolidating farms, readjusting debts and opening up to all comers many of the blocks that had been abandoned. Apart from its rehabilitation purposes it was to also a belated attempt to save the Crown the huge financial outlay it had originally made on the Soldier Settlers' Scheme.

In 1934 Jack Probert's farm, now called 'Warrawong' (Aboriginal for 'on the side of a hill') was reassessed and its original valuation of £1/5/6 an acre was dropped to 17/6. But in the long run the change made no difference. It simply postponed the inevitable. The

Jack and Nora on their property, Warrawong, and the log house in its completed form.

unforgiving seasons, the low crop yields and the uneconomic prices received for primary products through the decade provided little opportunity for Jack to get ahead.

Things were little better in 1935, although at the end of the year Jack purchased a further 200 sheep in an attempt to extend the farm. Once again there was a pitiful return of 22 bags of wheat after a dry summer, and the oat crop was a total failure. Whenever possible Jack and Nora continued to agist both sheep and cattle. The sheep produced three bales of wool. A few lambs were carted to Griffith and sold, while the turkeys brought in some very useful additional money. It was early in this year that Nora lost her first child.

Substantial and regular rain fell throughout 1936, but though the 735 mm they received almost trebled the district's normal rainfall, it proved in the long term an aberration. Nevertheless it filled the tank, feed became plentiful and by the end of the year Jack gambled on the apparent break to the drought to increase his flock to over 500 ewes and lambs. In doing so he also almost trebled the farm's previous year's return with the sale of the wool alone. He was able to deliver by horse lorry 23 bales of wool to the railhead at Rankins Springs, which sold at an average of 16 pence a pound. A substantial number of lambs were also sold at a reasonable 19/- each, and Jack was able to continue to have posts and strainers cut from his block and delivered to contractors in Bilbul and Yanco for a good return. In May Nora gave birth to a son, Sherriff, in Woodlands Private Hospital in Griffith.

The following year, 1937 was really the beginning of the end of farming for Jack. After a heavy fall of rain in early January there was little more over the next two years. Feed dried up, sheep lost condition and Jack was forced to buy lucerne for hand feeding. With continued hot dry weather he was forced to find money to pay a drover to put 150 of his sheep out in the 'long paddock' (roadside grazing). As the year went by he began to lose ewes to what is referred to in his farm journal as 'lamb sickness'. This appears to have been caused by the gradual build up of toxemia in pregnant ewes due to a deficiency in protein, resulting in the loss of both ewe and lamb. Jack lost nearly a third of his flock. Despite the sale of 11 bales of

*Griffith in the 1930s.
Above, the wide
streetscape. Centre,
the main street,
Banna Avenue.
Below, the Victoria
Hotel, Jack's
watering hole.*

*Photos courtesy
Griffith Genealogical
and Historical Society*

The converted hospital in Banna Avenue where Jack moved the family.

wool, 123 lambs and some agistment income, the drought was now biting into the farm's capacity to provide a living.

The final years on 'Warrawong' were soul-destroying. Jack's debt to Dalgetys had grown to an unmanageable size and he was forced in the last few months to regularly return sheep to Dalgetys to try and reduce the debt. But no sheep equalled no income, and the farm rapidly lost viability. Similar difficulties faced most of the other farmers, and the district's farming population shrank alarmingly. By the end of the 1930s almost two-thirds of the original pioneer soldier settlers had relinquished their farms and left the district.

In October 1938, after fourteen years of hard, unrelenting and grafting work, the Probert family were finally forced to join those who had already left. They simply walked off their farm and moved to Griffith. The final move was made a little easier at the time by the Government's offer of £300 to encourage farmers to leave unviable farms and find other ways to make a living. The intention was to help those who stayed by consolidating the remaining farms, and, with better economies of scale, give them some chance of surviving. Nevertheless, 'Warrawong' remained untenanted for ten years before it was finally purchased by Frank Mackay in 1948.

Jack found accommodation for his family in an old converted hospital building (now restored in the Griffith Pioneer Park) in the main

Jack becomes a merchant in Griffith. The Probert store (unidentified man).

street, Banna Avenue. After a short while he used the Government's incentive payment to rent commercial premises in Yambil Street. Early the following year Jack opened a small farmers' produce store in the hope of making a new beginning. In November 1939, John, their second son was born.

With the declaration of war Jack's plans for the future had to be put on hold. He was once again about to begin a dramatic new phase of his life.

CHAPTER 7

Second Time Around

When war broke out in late 1939 Jack was still establishing his small general produce and grain business in Griffith. Because of his World War 1 experience and his deep-seated conviction that Australia would eventually be drawn into a war to support the British, he offered himself as an instructor to the small local militia group, itself a part of the larger 56 Riverina Militia Regiment. At this time Australia had only a very small professional army of around 2,800 permanent soldiers. This was supplemented by 80,000 militia, consisting of part-time soldiers, men who held ordinary jobs during the week but spent some nights and weekends doing basic training, and attended annual camps. Even at this early stage it was becoming clear that Jack, just short of his 46th birthday, was being drawn into war once again.

For much of the 1930s the turmoil brewing in Europe was watched by most Australians with a somewhat detached interest. Even when war eventually broke out in September 1939 and the fighting in Europe was reported by Australian newspapers and radio, it still seemed such a long way off. For most Australians the attitude was simply 'business as usual'.

At first only a small number of men enlisted to serve overseas – some for patriotic reasons, others driven by a search for adventure. However by mid 1940, as the seriousness of the conflict in Europe grew, more Australians began to speak of joining up as their duty. Yet the number of men volunteering to serve overseas grew only slowly, and the Australian Government became concerned that Australians were not taking sufficient interest in the War effort.

All this was to change dramatically for Australians when Japan entered the war in December 1941.

Jack the Griffith businessman. With Nora and Sherriff in 1939.

Jack's first 'enlistment'

In late April 1940, after weeks of careful consideration, Jack decided to volunteer for army service. He was 46, and according to the Australian Army's clear stipulation exceeded the enlistment age by nearly seven years. Nevertheless he travelled from his home in Griffith to Caulfield, Victoria – near the suburb where he had been born – and enlisted in the Australian army claiming to be twelve years younger than he really was.

As soon as he was taken on strength he was appointed Acting Sergeant and posted to the Australian Army Corps Headquarters in Melbourne. A month later he was transferred as Acting Warrant

Departure of RMS Strathallan *from Melbourne, August 1940. Used as a troop transport, this ship took Jack to the Middle East soon after his first enlistment.*

Officer to the Army Intelligence Unit in the Corps Headquarters in Melbourne. Mid-way through August he was sent with the unit on RMS *Strathallan* for service in the Middle East.

And here remains a small, unresolved mystery. Within a month of landing in Suez and reporting to his unit in Gaza on 30 September 1940, he was suddenly demoted to the rank of private, transferred back to the transit unit at Suez, and by the end of November was returning to Australia on the troopship *Aquitania*. He arrived in Melbourne on 31 January 1941, was charged with a minor infraction involving an AWOL misdemeanour on the return trip (for leaving the ship on New Year's Eve in Durban in South Africa), and then formally discharged from the Army in Melbourne on 4 February 1941 – although according to Army records, 'not on account of misconduct'. Because of unexplained gaps in his service file, an educated guess would be that Jack Probert's real age had somehow surfaced, and the army had found itself obliged to return him to Australia and dismiss him from the services. On his service file there are brief references to letters from the legal arm of the Army, but

Jack and mates enjoy a beer in Tel Aviv, 1940. Little is known of Jack's first enlistment.

the letters and the details are missing and the real reasons for his discharge remain elusive.

A second bite at the cherry

Ignoring this setback, within two months of his discharge Jack enlisted a second time. This time he used the name 'John Moule-Probert' (his former Royal Flying Corps name), owned up to no previous army service and claimed to be only 39, just slightly older than he had claimed when he enlisted in Melbourne twelve months previously. He was now a 'thirty-nine liar'.* To further cover his tracks Jack travelled to an enlistment centre in Paddington, Sydney, and using a fancy new signature enlisted as a lowly gunner in the 2/15th Field Regiment, a newly formed unit of the Eighth Division of the Second AIF.

This field artillery regiment had been raised from scratch in the latter part of 1940, just a year prior to its first engagement with the Japanese in the jungles of Malaya in December 1941. It started with nothing but raw recruits and a few trained officers drawn somewhat

---

* Army regulations stipulated that enlisting men were to be no older than 39. Many older men simply dropped their age to 39 or less in order join up. They became known as 'thirty-nine liars'.

Jack on his final leave in 1941, with his two young sons, Sherriff and John.

resentfully from established Australian regiments. It began as a tent camp on a large open paddock just outside Ingleburn west of Sydney, but early in the following year moved to a more established camp at Holsworthy.

In the months prior to its embarkation for Singapore in July 1941 the new regiment was subjected to an arduous and intensive training program. Jack did not join training until 21 May, by which time the Holsworthy program was well advanced. Instead he was sent to the First Field Training Regiment in Cowra in southern NSW where similar military preparations were also being carried out. On 10 July the regiment received notice to prepare for its first overseas posting. Three weeks later, in the early morning of 29 July 1941, Jack found himself, along with hundreds of other soldiers, at Sydney's Darling Harbour preparing to embark for a destination which the troops could only guess at.

Later that morning he boarded the *Johan van Oldenbarnevelt,*

Jack's own photograph of troops on the deck of the Johan van Oldenbarnevelt, *August 1941, bound for Singapore.*

a small, former coastal steamer newly converted to a troop transport, about which the troops complained that the hammocks hung so closely together that men who left them at night for any reason had enormous difficulty finding them again! As Jack's ship sailed under the Sydney Harbour Bridge and down the harbour in the late afternoon sun, the *Oldenbarnevelt* was joined by two other troop ships, the *Katoomba* and the *Marnix van St Aldegonde*, and a short while later by a small RAN cruiser escort. The tiny convoy passed through the Heads, swung right and headed slowly down the south coast of NSW.

Early days in Malaya

After two weeks at sea (with a brief stop-over in Fremantle) the convoy reached its destination, Singapore, on 15 August 1941. The trip proved uneventful, and the troops were kept fully occupied during most days with endless lectures and drills. In the long evenings, to escape the slowly ascending temperature and humidity of the tropics, they spent much of their spare time on the decks smoking, yarning and contemplating their destination. When the convoy passed into the Java Straits the men experienced their first taste of the war they were entering. Their evenings had to be spent in the dark as the ships blacked out all lights for fear of Japanese submarines.

Hut scrubbing day with members of D Troop, November 1941.

The new arrivals were met on the Singapore docks by fellow Australian troops who had arrived in February in an initial Australian convoy aboard the famous *Queen Mary.* They were quickly trucked to a newly tented area at Nee Soon close to the British barracks where, unlike the experience of the previous Australian troops, everything was ready for them.

At first many of the men saw themselves as having been sent to Singapore only for garrison duty. There was no real conviction that they would have to confront the enemy; after all, the conventional wisdom was that Singapore was impregnable. Along with this sense of invincibility they felt deep disappointment. As many of the troops saw it, the real action was in the Middle East. A similar impression also grew in Australia, where in the weeks following their arrival, distorted reports in the newspapers and on the radio described the 'high and easy life' the troops were leading in Singapore. As a result, in some quarters they were labelled somewhat disparagingly as the 'glam' boys, who were having the time of their lives while other Australian boys were fighting for theirs in the deserts of the Middle East. Some soldiers even experienced the ignominy of receiving anonymous letters containing white feathers.

Nevertheless, the early weeks in Singapore *were* different from what many might have expected. Most took advantage of the numerous clamouring Indian boys, who for a small weekly reimbursement would tidy tents, make beds and clean boots. They took regular leave in the city, explored the narrow streets, bartered with the Indian traders and drank beer at the many small hotels they found in the back streets of Singapore. For most of these young Australians, this was their first experience outside their suburb or country town, let alone a foreign country. It was their first contact with a different culture.

Jack's regiment quickly settled into a pattern of work and play. It took delivery of vehicles released from the battlefields of the Middle East – painted an incongruous, rich, desert-yellow! The soldiers repainted their vehicles and began practising convoy-driving along the narrow roads that criss-crossed the island. They sweated profusely in the equatorial climate, and more often than not went about their duties shirtless. They quickly discovered that, away from the city, the island was still extensively covered with jungle, with floors of dense foliage. Nevertheless it was a valuable period, used to work the regiment into a state of readiness.

On 10 September 1941 came the long-awaited move up-country to Tampin, on the border of the state of Malacca some 240 kilometres north-west of Singapore. As a driver of one of the numerous 30 cwt (1.5 tonne) trucks of the 30th Battery used for carrying stores, guns and ammunition, Jack helped ferry the regiment to their new scene of operations. They found a camp with airy huts, a canteen serving light meals and local ales, and a free laundry service. And for the first time the troops experienced much of what their commissioned officers took for granted – most of the camp fatigues carried out by locals.

In late September 1941, a couple of weeks after the move to Tampin, the camp experienced a sudden outbreak of mumps. Jack was among many of his battery to have an enforced stay in the Australian General Hospital in the town of Malacca, a few kilometres west of Tampin. After three weeks in hospital, another three weeks at the Convalescent Depot and a period at General Battalion Headquarters, he rejoined his battery at Tampin on 14 November, finding considerable changes had occurred in his absence. The battery had received its first British-made 25-pound howitzers and the men had made eager progress in mastering the guns' intricacies. More significant, however, was the realisation among the men that war with Japan was now just around the corner. Jack had in fact rejoined his battery only just in time to help pack to leave Tampin.

On 6 December Jack drove his truck in a convoy several miles long south-west through the narrow, winding, hilly roads to the Mengkibol Rubber Estate, where his Battery's task was to defend the Kluang airstrip. Unbeknown to the men, every available Allied contingent throughout the Malayan peninsula was now being posted to action stations in preparation for the Japanese onslaught that was to begin in a matter of hours.

There was not long to wait. Two nights later, in the early hours of the morning, Singapore, with its lights blazing, the dance bands playing, the cafes, restaurants and clubs in full swing, received its first unwanted visitors. The Japanese bombed the city, letting the world know that the war in the Pacific had begun. It was 8 December 1941, the same day Pearl Harbor, on the other side of the dateline, was also attacked.

A baptism of fire

While the move by the Australians to take up defensive positions at the Kluang aerodrome and township had been swift and efficient, for the next couple of weeks of December nothing happened. Time dragged slowly and tensely. Cocooned in their new defensive locations the men knew little of the rapid progress that the Japanese were making down the peninsula. Nothing could be done: they just had to wait. Then, quite unexpectedly, at noon on 29 December they heard the sound of approaching aircraft, and out of the north-east fifteen Japanese bombers emerged and proceeded to pockmark the airstrip and its surrounding encampment with huge 500 pound bombs. In a letter home to his wife a couple of days later Jack wrote:

> Sorry I have been unable to write since Christmas but had no hope at all. Been flat out ever since. The Jap is giving us the works from the air ... We had a nice little raid ourselves as a New Year's gift. He dropped about 50 bombs round us and missed his target by feet, thank God. Then the swine turned and machine gunned the town and didn't hit a cat ... Of course I felt as windy as hell and was waiting for one to drop on the truck. I was parked

on the side of the road and elected to sit tight in the bus rather than dash for the drain.

Anyhow we are all safe and well and have gone through a kind of baptism of fire. The boys are tickled to death coz it wipes the 'garrison glamour boy' business that was wished on the Malayan troops. We reckon we have just as big a job here now as they have in the Middle East.

There was a further air raid on 5 January, this time at dawn. 'They don't want us to sleep in', the gunners grumbled. But sleep was something that had to be grabbed in small doses whenever possible. Then on 9 January the order came: 'We leave at dawn for the north.'

Gunner in the jungle
In trying to recreate this section of Jack's story these few letters that he wrote to his wife in the midst of the Malayan campaign were the only source we had. But these letters initially presented a problem. While they painted a vivid picture of Jack's experience – the interruptions as diving Japanese planes dropped bombs on Jack's troop, the smells and sounds of battle, the fear and anxiety as the Japanese infiltrated behind the Australian lines during the night, even some wry Australian humour as he compares himself to a farm rabbit diving into the slit trenches – they had been carefully censored, and therefore we knew neither the actions in which he was engaged nor his exact position.

Thankfully the answer came in the form of Cliff Whitelocke's *Gunners in the Jungle*, the official history of the 2/15th Field Regiment. Using field diaries and interviews with members of the Regiment, Whitelocke methodically reconstructed the Regiment's Malayan campaign. For us it became a matter of systematically aligning the content of Jack's letters with Whitelocke's history of the 2/15th's campaign trail. The letters now made sense.

The move north
The move north was to lead to the regiment's first military action. The stores were packed and a convoy of 24 guns and 130 vehicles set out. As they drove towards Yong Peng they met roads jammed with

A letter from Jack to his wife, written in the midst of a Japanese air attack, January 1942.

1089 & Gnr.
J. Maule-Probert
2/15 th. Field Regt.
A.I.F.
Malaya

16-1-42

In the rubber
plane
with Japs overhead.

Hullo Modgie - so sorry that I have not been able to write before - chucked now, he's gone now - jee the cow came back & almost on top of us. sure he saw us. Any how he laid a few eggs but all is well. You no doubt know now that we've been in it. Contacted the swine yesterday morning, & our chaps gave him larry dooley. It said a few were missing - well the missing wandered in this morning, about 11 ams. Between us we accounted for about 4oo Japs & we only had two minor casualties. Of course I can't write much now Modgie but this is to let you know that I'm still safe & well. Get the jitters of course but we all do that. A lot of bombing,

135

Indian and British troops withdrawing south. These retreating troops had borne the full brunt of the Japanese in their sweep down the west coast and were exhausted. They had fought rearguard actions without respite, and almost no air support. Nevertheless as the Australians headed north they were excited that at long last they were about to engage the enemy and put their months of training to the test.

For the next three days the Australian convoy was masked from Japanese air reconnaissance by low cloud and heavy rain which gave them good cover. At Yong Peng the 65th Battery swung west to join the 45th Indian Brigade, to eventually confront the oncoming Japanese at the River Muar in what was to become one of the bloodiest defeats for the Allies in the Malayan campaign. Jack and his 30th Battery continued north towards Gemas.

On 13 January they reached their designated positions just five kilometres west of the town of Gemas and dug in. The Australians met with early success. In their first engagement with the Japanese they effectively ambushed a large force of advancing Japanese just outside Gemas where a small bridge crossed the Sungei Gemencheh. The ambush party had waited 48 hours for a large party of Japanese cyclists to cross the bridge, oblivious to what was in store. As they moved laughing and chattering across the bridge and into the steep cutting below under the gaze of the waiting Australians, the order was given. The bridge and all the Japanese soared skywards. From each side of the cutting the remaining enemy troops were methodically cut down by devastating fire from machine guns and rifles. By the time the order to retire was given, not a living Japanese remained on the road.

While the vanguard had been wiped out, days of vicious fighting followed as the Japanese moved in over 2,000 reinforcements. Japanese war historians later described the action that followed as one 'fought with a bravery we had not previously seen'. The Australians were caught in a bitter holding action. Each night there were heavy exchanges of shells, the safest place for the troops being the nearest slit trench. During the day Japanese aircraft flew constant sorties searching for the infantry and destroying all the gun placements they could find. At the same time Dutch bombers, escorted by a handful

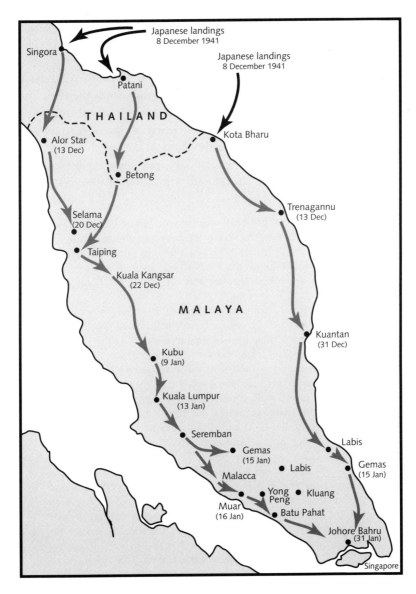

Routes taken by Japanese forces along the Malay Peninsula in 1941–1942, leading up to the capture of Singapore.

of Australian fighters, did great damage to the hundreds of Japanese supply trucks that had piled up on the road behind the action. The Australians suffered 80 casualties, of whom 17 were killed.

The Australian ambush at Gemas resulted in a temporary setback for the enemy. For the first time in their advance down the coast the Japanese had been forced to reassess their strategy – as a result they quickly switched large numbers of their troops to the west to try and create an alternative route across the River Muar and then south. In a letter to the family dated 16 January, put together in snatches during this fighting, Jack wrote, with a measure of bravado, of his experiences:

> So sorry that I have not been able to write before – cheeky cow, he's gone now – gee, the cow came back and almost on top of us – sure he saw us. Anyhow he laid a few eggs but all is well.
>
> You no doubt know that we've been in it. Contacted the swine again yesterday morning and our chaps gave him larry dooley ...
>
> Between us we accounted for about 400 Japs and we had only two minor casualties. Of course I can't write much now but this is to let you know that I'm still safe and well. Get the jitters of course but we all do that. A lot of bombing makes one jumpy naturally. Diving into drains and slit trenches or what have you about a dozen times a day gives you the jumps in time.
>
> I just started to write you this when we got the aircraft signal. I continued to write my address coz I knew he was past, but the little cow turned around and dived at us so I dived under the truck. Well wouldn't it! Another's arrived – hence another dive for cover. Life is certainly exciting, Nodgie ...
>
> We've been having a few sleepless nights and wet days lately – another rainy season passing ... it isn't a front line here where you know where the enemy is. He infiltrates and he is apt to come in from anywhere in the dark and we all have to do our patrols in pairs and the nights are pitch black. My nerves are standing up to it well so far
>
> Damn, I hear another plane. Our ears are highly attuned now believe me.

It was clear that the Japanese build-up of forces around Gemas was strengthening. After a week of bitter fighting the Australians

Japanese troops in the vicinity of Gemas, 14/1/1942. A heavily camouflaged Japanese Type 97 Tankette near Gemas, 17/1/1942.

were forced to fall back. Through difficult terrain and sodden ground the 29th and 30th Batteries leap-frogged each other, covering each other as they moved towards the town of Segamat. It rained incessantly and the conditions were abysmal. Vans, ammunition trucks and Bren carriers became bogged. As they fell back they blew bridges to delay the enemy, but in the chaos of withdrawal there were many communication breakdowns. They were often given orders that were just as quickly countermanded. The Japanese aircraft continued to search out and destroy a number of the artillery guns and vehicles, and with the Japanese routinely penetrating their lines and creating havoc, the men were often unsure where their own lines were.

By 19 January the Australian forces retreating from Gemas reached Segamat. The following day they established a new position at Labis, where they were asked at all costs to keep open the road from Muar to allow as many as possible of the struggling, exhausted survivors of the battle of the River Muar to reach safety. In the midst of this fighting Jack continued his correspondence to his wife:

> I haven't heard from you but I suppose all our mail is at base and cannot be brought to us ... Been in and out of action twice to date and I don't know which is to be preferred really – in the line with the Japs all around us or back a bit, being bombed every half hour by their planes. If only they would come at us from the front ... but they won't, they infiltrate at night and get all around us – it is a kind of guerilla war all the time.
>
> ... I'm safe and well so far – just a bit nervy of course. Strung up really but that is to be expected ... We were first into action and are still in. I'm writing this on my knee in the truck between air raids. We all dig slit trenches to dive into but this position we are in I have commandeered a big bricked in oven which was used to smoke rubber and I can just fit in. Saves a lot of hard digging.
>
> ... We always move at night into positions and out. Sleep is the hardest thing to get for you can't sleep for the noise of our guns at night and part of the day and the other part of the day you can't for air attacks.

It was clear by this time that the peninsular war was over for the Allies. They were rapidly running out of land. The Japanese pressure was mounting and daytime travel was becoming increasingly hazardous. Finally, on 20 January the decision was made by the Allied High Command and plans put in place for a final withdrawal of all Allied troops into Singapore.

It would appear that in the very last days of the mainland campaign Jack suffered a minor injury, or perhaps a touch of malaria that led to his evacuation to hospital for a couple of days. He wrote briefly:

> Am in hospital and still quite safe. Have been in action up to last Sunday for a solid fortnight. The dive bombing was by far the worst part of the show. Was evacuated to hospital ... nerves are a little frayed and am gone in the legs but otherwise OK ...
>
> ... the age is telling a bit and it is hard having to admit it, but these conditions so test one out.
>
> Just had a substantial air raid. It's a war from the air alright nowadays ...

AWM 012449

An Australian anti-tank gun emplacement in Singapore overlooking the Johore causeway at the Japanese buildup on the Malayan shore, just before the invasion of Singapore.

> Let me tell you that the rabbit has nothing on me. If you saw me diving into holes when the Japs come over in their fighters you'd realise it too.

By the time Jack rejoined D Troop a few days later it had already moved to the 16 mile peg (25 km) just outside Johore Bahru prior to its final dash into Singapore itself. From here, late in the evening of 29 January, D troop with the help of local guides moved quietly onto side tracks that led through the darkness of the villages and the countryside to the causeway. Luck was with the troops in more ways than one. By the time the troops had reached the causeway it had become a clear moonlit night, and had the Japanese been more venturesome with their night flying operations they could have inflicted enormous damage on the withdrawing columns. The routes to the causeway were jammed with equipment and vehicles stacked bumper

Lihatlah kĕlakuan soldadu-soldadu dari Australia yang tĕrlalu
amat kĕbĕngisannya.

Gambar ini tĕrlukis tangan bumiputĕra Mĕlayu yang dibunoh olehnya.

*A propaganda leaflet dropped over Malayan towns and villages by
the Japanese pointing out that Australians cut the wrists of Malayans
and left them to bleed to death. The leaflet was included in a letter
Jack sent to his family in January 1942.*

to bumper for kilometres. Fortunately the roads and dirt tracks were
quite dry as no rain had fallen for days.

When they finally reached the safety of the island of Singapore the
Australians had been fighting almost continuously for three weeks.

The fall of Singapore

The island of Singapore had two main defensive advantages. The first
was the narrow stretch of water cutting it off from the mainland, and
the second the terrain of the island. The latter provided the defence
installations with shelter and natural camouflage which limited observation from the air. But there were also three-quarters of a million
defenceless civilians on the island to be fed, housed and looked after.

The siege began the day part of the causeway was blown up,
31 January. Shelling was sporadic for the first few days and the
Australian command, not content to sit back and let the Japanese to
do all the attacking, sent small night patrols over to the mainland
to observe. They reported heavy concentrations of the enemy on the

142

coast and in the jungles of the high country further back. However, the information did not reach Percival, the Allied Commander, and he persisted in the conviction that the Japanese would attempt a landing in the north-east sector.

It was a puzzling and frustrating time for the Australian troops. They could actually see the enemy across the water, and the Japanese in turn could watch the movement of individual men through their binoculars. In the week that followed there was considerable Japanese artillery and mortar fire, and daytime travel became very hazardous. Their long-range batteries shelled the city, adding to the growing havoc caused by the heavy pattern-bombing over both the city and the docks. Yet most people in Singapore tried to carry on with their normal lives, even protesting at the thought of evacuation.

The battle for Singapore opened seven days after the siege had begun, on 8 February. The troops had been grimly waiting for the inevitable invasion, and during the night of 8 February over 13,000 Japanese troops landed on the north-west perimeter using light landing craft. Defending units were scattered widely enough for the enemy to quickly thrust between them. Many had no chance. Nor could other units be moved up because this would leave another sector undefended. The Japanese had only one thing in mind: Singapore. When they were baulked at one point they concentrated on another. The Australian defenders were left with kilometres of coastline to defend.

At first light on the morning of 9 February the British commander finally realised that he had been wrong and transferred some British troops into the Australians' area, but they arrived too late to stem the flow of Japanese onto the island. By midday on 11 February, the defences were in confusion. The end was fast approaching.

The confusion that marks this period makes it difficult to trace Jack's movements. His return from hospital to rejoin D Troop just outside Johore Bahru seems to have coincided with orders to evacuate. All vehicles, trucks and gun carriers were sent to Singapore while D troop remained behind. They continued to be heavily engaged, up to midnight on 30 January, in directing harassing fire at enemy positions to provide cover for retreating troops. An educated guess is that

AWM 011303/29

Australian troops alighting from a truck during the Allied retreat to Singapore

Jack, as a driver, was in Singapore with his truck just prior to his Troop returning over the causeway to take up its defensive position close to the Tengah aerodrome. It was probably here that he linked up with them again. This would account for the story, reported by Jack's half-brother Charles and sourced from a mutual friend who saw it happen, that, as the Australians retreated across the causeway, Jack was seen at the end of it with the Melbourne Grammar School emblem emblazoned in burnt cork across his bare chest, greeting troops with toddies of rum to help them on their way.

During the following few days of the battle for Singapore roads, tracks, junctions and likely troop placements around the Tengah aerodrome were systematically shelled. Shells dropped everywhere around the Troop's gun placements, and as the bombardment intensified it became virtually impossible to leave the protection of the slit trenches. D Troop was reported to have suffered heavy casualties to

144

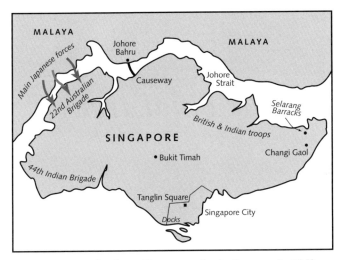

Singapore at the time of its capture by the Japanese in 1942.

vehicles and guns, and on 9 February, when the final withdrawal to the city itself was ordered, its losses were so great that in the following reorganisation D Troop ceased to exist, its remnants being absorbed into other troops. Until the capitulation of the Allies a week later, Jack's movements, like thousands of other dejected troops who had no special responsibility, can only be guessed.

In the three days before the Allied surrender the Japanese attacked Singapore with renewed vigour. The merciless bombing raids continued to inflict enormous damage and caused heavy casualties among the civilian population. Almost to the minute, every half-hour three groups each of 27 bombers came in perfect formation over the city, and at a given signal, all the planes released their bombs. The 'whoosh' of hundreds of bombs falling together became a familiar and ominous sound.

On 15 February Percival found his position untenable and that night formally surrendered to the Japanese. The Malayan campaign was over.

CHAPTER 8

The Final Irony

At the fall of Singapore. Jack Probert was interned along with 15,000 other Australian soldiers in the Selarang Barracks on the Changi peninsula east of Singapore, while the 37,000 British, along with the Indian and Dutch prisoners, were held a little further down the peninsula in the Roberts, Kitchener and India Barracks.

The Australian troops spent much of this early period of captivity in work details, cleaning up the rubble and mess, burying bodies, and, under Japanese supervision, restoring a semblance of order to the city after the massive destruction that preceded the Allied surrender. Thousands of troops, many of them Australians, were sent to work on ambitious projects like the building of a Shinto temple and the construction of a War Memorial near the village of Bukit Timah.

It was here that Jack, upholding the finest traditions of the Australian army, was reported by Dick Braithwaite, one of the six survivors of Sandakan, to have 'borrowed' the local village post office clock, stuffed it into his kitbag and succeeded in keeping its presence hidden, much to the amusement of all who knew about it. It is not known how long the 'souvenir' was retained or what ends it may have served, but the feat created a great deal of admiration among his fellow troops at the time.

In a series of interviews with Tim Bowden from the ABC in 1984, Braithwaite relates another incident involving Jack. He recalls that within a week of capitulation to the Japanese, the Australian troops were quite unexpectedly called for a full dress parade to be inspected by a visiting British General. Understandably, the Australian troops

AWM 043917

Selarang Barracks, Changi, later in the war (January 1943) after Jack had been sent to Borneo. This photograph shows a parade held to celebrate Australia Day.

expressed resentment at this seemingly empty gesture of maintaining appearances. Braithwaite recalls that as the general moved along the ranks:

> He passed this little fellow a couple from me. He did a double take and went back and he questioned [Jack], pointing to his chest and I heard him say, 'That's an MC ribbon you have there, soldier.'
>
> And this fellow said, 'Yes sir.'
>
> He said, 'Where did you get that?'
>
> He said, 'With the Royal Flying Corps in World War One.'
>
> And with that he looked a bit nonplussed and walked on shaking his head, probably thinking, 'Colonials! Putting Royal Flying officers in the ranks!'

馬來

便 郵 虜 俘

Sce DES PRISONNIERS DE GUERRE

PASSED BY CENSOR 423

俘虜收容所
檢閱濟

Mʳˢ J. MOULE-PROBERT

GRIFFITH, NEW SOUTH WALES,

AUSTRALIA

岡崎

JOHN MOULE-PROBERT. NX10894. GUNNER

MY DEAR WIFE, 20 JUNE 1942

I AM A PRISONER OF WAR. AT

PRESENT AM FIT AND FEELING

WELL. FONDEST LOVE TO YOURSELF

AND THE CHILDREN.

J. Moule-Probert.

Jack Probert's first postcard home two weeks before 'B' Force left Singapore for North Borneo on 4 July 1942.

The official
telegram
informing
Jack's family
of his capture
arrived on
1 March 1943,
a year after
the event.

FUNDS MAY BE QUICKLY, SAFELY AND ECONOMICALLY TRANSFERRED BY
MONEY ORDER TELEGRAM.
(PLEASE TURN OVER.)

COMMONWEALTH OF AUSTRALIA · POSTMASTER-GENERAL'S DEPARTMENT.

RECEIVED TELEGRAM

The first line of this telegram contains the following particulars in the order named.

Office of Origin.   Words.   Time Lodged.   No.

Victoria Barracks Sydney   45   1.15

Remarks.   Sch. C.2106 - 10/1939

To Mrs Lora Moule-Probert
46 Harbord Rd
Harbord

Gunner Moule Probert - Prisoner of War.
I have to inform you that N.X 10894
Gunner John Moule Probert - previously
reported missing is now reported
prisoner of war interned Borneo
Camp.
Minister for the Army.

148

In the months after the fall of Singapore anxious families in Australia received little news in the newspapers or on the radio that was not carefully vetted for public consumption. It was a painful period, and for some families lasted up to eighteen months before news of the fate of their menfolk was received. Cards sent by the prisoners had to pass through the Red Cross in Tokyo and then Geneva before being received by the Red Cross in Australia.

Confirmation that Jack had at least survived the battle of Singapore and become a prisoner of the Japanese arrived in Griffith in the form of a solitary postcard, dated 20 June 1942, in the early months of 1943, almost a year after it had been sent from the Selarang Barracks. Four months after the Allied surrender, the Japanese had relented and allowed the Australian prisoners to send their first messages home. The postcards were restricted to 25 words and were required by the Japanese to be written in large, clear block letters. Necessarily brief and impersonal, this postcard represented to the family the first sign that Jack had survived.

In early 1942 the 'eye' of the Japanese invasion passed Singapore, and the following months were used by the Japanese, in co-operation with senior Allied officers, in organising prisoners into a number of separate forces for local and overseas draft. At the beginning of their incarceration groups of Australians were distributed in work parties all over Singapore. In mid-May 'A' Force comprising 3,000 men was sent to Thailand. With the departure of these and other work groups the Australian POWs remaining at Selarang mostly comprised the sick, the convalescent, those on light duties, the less well disciplined, the older men, those engaged in running the camp, and a large number of officers and warrant officers not required to work.

On 4 July the Japanese announced the need for a further draft of 2,000 prisoners to leave for overseas within three days. Only when the Japanese came to assemble the group did they realise the difficulty in filling such a quota with able-bodied men. Forced to set a lower target of 1,500, the Japanese filled the quota of 'volunteers' only by convincing the camp administration that the men were destined for a convalescent camp overseas where there would be nourishing food, plenty of medical supplies and the promise of only light duties. Three

Gnr. J. Moule-Probert

His War Service

Under the heading "Four Dip—in War," "Reveille" prints the following concerning Gnr. J. Moule-Probert, Griffith:—

In a recent Malayan casualty list there is the name of Gnr. J. Moule-Probert (Art.)

In England, with his father, in August 1914, Johnny, at the age of 17, joined the B.E.F., reached France in September 1914, "boxed on" until taken prisoner at Looe in November, 1915.

After 14 months in a P.O.W. camp in Western Germany, he escaped with a mate to Blighty—through Finland, Sweden and Norway.

After a month's leave, he joined the R.A.F., and, on being shot down on Armistice morning, he finished up with the M.C. and C. de G., and a plate in the head.

After years as a south-western farmer, he was in an agency in Griffith at the outbreak of the present war.

As he was on the Reserve of Officers, he was called up, and proceeded to the Middle East as a W.O. 1.

At Benghazi he suffered shock after a bombing raid, and, on being invalided home, was discharged as unfit for further service.

Six weeks passed, and Johnny was again found in the A.I.F., this time as a gunner in the 2/15 Field Regt., R.A.A., whith which he was serving when Singapore fell.

Here's hoping he can, if a prisoner, find his way home, as in the first Stunt.—K.G.

This report appeared in the Area News, *a local Griffith newspaper, on 2 October, eight months after Jack's capture.*

While expressing a touching concern for a local indentity, it also illustrates how difficult it has been to sort fact from fiction in recreating Jack's life. The report has the broad gist of Jack's adventures correct, but very little of the factual detail.

days later Jack left with 'B' Force on the *Yubi Maru* for an unknown destination. It proved to be Sandakan, in the jungles of North Borneo.

Information on Jack's time in Sandakan has not been easy to uncover. Apart from four of the most formal and brief of Japanese POW postcards, little information was received by the family of Jack's whereabouts and his condition. Almost no information was received by any of the families of these Sandakan prisoners during this three-year period. It was not until late 1942 – months after their capture in Singapore – that even the sketchiest intelligence about the whereabouts of these soldiers became known to the Australian Army. Even then it took the Army some time to pass on this information, and the official censorship policies of the time prevented the media from publishing it.

When peace was declared in August 1945 and official notifications of the fate of soldiers were sent to next of kin, Australian families still found extreme difficulty in getting any detailed personal information about the fate of their family members. Only the very faintest glimpse was allowed to emerge of the horrors these soldiers endured.

Yet as soon as North Borneo was liberated by the Australians, a diligent and comprehensive investigation of Sandakan was carried out by the Army. Substantial information was assembled of the camp life of these prisoners from reports of those who had survived, as well as from the locals who had assisted the prisoners with food and medical help, even though under constant threat of reprisals and death from the Japanese. Fragments of personal belongings which survived the ravages of the jungle, either in the camp or along the route of the death marches, were collected, and when identified, were sent to their families. Yet much of the detailed information assembled in the months immediately following the end of the war was not made available.

Similarly, little of the detail of the atrocities and deprivations assembled and presented to the Borneo War Crime trials filtered back to affected Australian families. Official policy was that the details were too shocking to release to the public, and the media were persuaded to endorse this policy.

Like hundreds of other families throughout Australia, the Probert family sought information about their kin by writing to the Army, as well as to the few who had survived the camp, but to little avail.

Then suddenly, after almost fifty years of knowing so little of Jack's fate, two events occurred within a short space of time that shed light on his experiences.

First was the fortuitous discovery, described at the beginning of this book, of the letter written by a Lieutenant Rod Wells to Jack's wife and only found recently in her estate papers. (The letter is reproduced on pages 152–153.) Rod Wells, a fellow prisoner of war in Sandakan, had struck up a close relationship with Jack, and in spite of

Lieutenant Rod W

3 Holyrood Av.
Nth Essendon,
27 Dec 45.

Dear Mrs Probert,

My wife and I extend to you our deepest sympathy in the loss of your husband John.

On 8th July 42 "B" Force, a party of 1500 Australian prisoners left Singapore for Sandakan, British North Borneo arriving on 18th July. A month or so after we arrived I was in charge of a work party under the Japs when by coincidence I met John by mentioning a mutual friend at Caulfield in early 1940. My father was an officer in 1914-18 and John knew some of his friends at the Naval & Military Club. By degrees we became very friendly, and I feel I almost know you and the boys from the stories John told me of his early days, the farm, meeting you etc. We sat together at night, boiled coffee, talked, planned to escape, discussed what we would do etc. Then John went to Hospital, I obtained a little fish etc from natives, gave him a little assistance. He got better, but then the boot was on the other foot.

Capt. L.C. Matthews a brother officer and I during this twelve months in question were running an espionage organization, contacting the Allies etc (quite an article about it in the first addition "Herald" Melbourne Cup Day Nov. 8 which I would like you to see). Matthews & I were arrested by the "Gestapo", tortured etc and eventually sentenced to death. I was later reprieved, sentenced to 12 years penal servitude in dungeon cells, my friend was executed.

... in Singapore. When
...3, we both thought
... return home.
..., but since I have
...stralian War Crimes
...details for Records of
...ct result of Japane
... effecting reprisals
...husband has been

...its, and if possible
... at Tatura. In
... guide your children
... as it is only by
... of the ~~...~~ beastial

nature of the Japanese that we can keep them down commercially politically and economically. My wife and I send you and yours our best wishes for the coming year under the circumstances.

Yours Sincerely,

Roderick G. Wells Lieut.

3 Holyrood Av.
North Essendon
27 Dec 45

Dear Mrs Probert

My wife and I extend to you our deepest sympathy in the loss of your husband John.

On 8th July 42 'B' Force, a party of 1500 Australian prisoners left Singapore for Sandakan, British North Borneo arriving on 18th July. A month or so after we arrived I was in charge of a work party under the Japs when by coincidence I met John by mentioning a mutual friend at Caulfield in early 1940. My father was an officer in 1914-18 and John knew some of his friends at the Naval and Military Club. By degrees we became very friendly, and I feel I almost know you and the boys from the stories John told me of his early days, the farm, meeting you, etc. We sat together at night, boiled coffee, talked, planned to escape, discussed what we would do, etc. Then John went to hospital, I obtained a little fish etc. from natives, gave him a little assistance. He got better, but then the boot was on the other foot.

Capt. L.C. Matthews, a brother officer and I during this twelve months in question were running an espionage organization, contacting the Allies etc., (quite an article about it in the first addition [sic] *Herald* Melbourne Cup Day Nov. 8 which I would like you to see). Matthews and I were arrested by the 'Gestapo', tortured etc and eventually sentenced to death. I was later reprieved, sentenced to 12 years penal servitude in dungeon cells; my friend was executed

I was lucky enough to be relieved before I died in Singapore. When John waved 'goodbye' to me on 24th July, 1943, we both thought it would be he and not me who would return home.

Please forgive me for not writing before, but since I have been back, I have been busy with the Australian War Crimes Commission, Military Intelligence and the details for Records of the men who died in Sandakan as a direct result of Japanese treatment. The giving of evidence in the hope of effecting reprisals against the murderers of men like your husband has been a big job, but a delightful one.

I hope to hear from you when time permits and if possible to see you. My people are on the land at Tatura. In closing, I hope you will do your best to guide your children along the lines of hatred for the enemy as it is only by making the coming generations conscious of the bestial nature of the Japanese that we can keep them down commercially, politically and economically. My wife and I send you and yours our best wishes for the coming year under the circumstances.

Yours sincerely

Roderick G. Wells Lieut.

incredible hardships and torture at the hands of the Kempei-tai (the Japanese military police), he had miraculously survived. Still alive, though frail in health, Wells is the sole living survivor of the Sandakan experience who actually knew Jack directly. His generous help has been invaluable in piecing together this unknown chapter of Jack's life.

The other significant event was the recent (1998) publication by Lynette Ramsay Silver of *Sandakan: A Conspiracy of Silence*. This book provides a painstaking and horrifying account of the lives and ultimate fate of the POWs who perished at Sandakan at the hands of the Japanese. It has been invaluable in completing the story of Jack's life.

From Singapore to Sandakan

The 1,500 Australian officers and men of 'B' Force spent 10 days in the fetid, airless holds of the rusty 1,500-tonne tramp steamer, *Yubi Maru*. Built for the Australian wheat trade, before the war it had been sold (along with several other Australian ships) by the Australian Prime Minister, Robert Menzies, to the Japanese for scrap (hence his sobriquet 'Pig Iron Bob'), but it had been retained as a collier by the Japanese to ply its domestic ports. The collier now entered a third life, transporting Australian prisoners of war for the Japanese.

In his 1983 interview with Tim Bowden, Dick Braithwaite provides a glimpse of the ship and the conditions experienced during the voyage:

> The *Yubi Maru* was a small freighter, I think about 1,500 tonnes, and I was told by someone who knew something about it, it was a ship that ... had been used in Australia, and had been scrapped ... But of course the Japanese turned it to use.
>
> Well, a 1,500 tonne ship, 1,500 prisoners, plus guards and crew and freight and so on, you can imagine it was pretty crowded. And in the forward holds that we were placed in there wasn't room to barely sit up, and there wasn't room for everyone to lie down at the same time, and of course it was stifling hot ... I don't recall any deaths on it, but it was very uncomfortable ... and the toilets were little outhouses slung over the side of the deck ... the food was pretty terrible, it was sulphurated rice and

The primitive sanitary facilities on the Yubi Maru. *Sketch by Bill Young.*

very occasionally some weed or weedy soup that went with it, but
the rice was ... was full of yellow stones and very gritty ...

Tim Bowden, interview with R. Braithwaite
from unedited transcripts, *Australia Under Nippon*,
Australian Broadcasting Corporation, 1983

There were in fact three holds, without portholes, and vertical
iron ladders up to the decks. The only ventilation was a canvas air
scoop funnelling into each of the holds – it only functioned when the
ship was moving. One of the holds was 10 centimetres deep in coal
dust, and into this were jammed 760 men. Along with 400 other
prisoners Jack found himself in the aft hold, cheek-by-jowl with
Braithwaite. Braithwaite recalls that during the long days and nights
of the voyage they maintained morale with card playing, yarning and
community singing.

In her book on Sandakan, Silver describes how Braithwaite,
remembering the incident with the British general, asked Jack to
share some of his stories with those in the rear hold:

> Squashed beside Braithwaite in the rear hold, [he] kept those
> around him spellbound with the story of his World War 1 experi-
> ences. [Jack] a 39-liar, was really 45 but had put his age back to
> 39 to enlist the second time around. He had served in the Great
> War with the Royal Flying Corps until he was shot down over

A panorama of the town of Sandakan, Borneo, 1941, at that time the capital of British North Borneo. Well-kept houses stand in neat rows along pleasant streets, there is an open sports field – the padang *– at the left, and the bay is visible in the background at right.*

German lines. He had polished up his schoolboy German while recovering, so that by the time he was discharged from hospital he was fluent. A very likeable and affable bloke, he was a great hit with his captors, who appointed him a Red Cross liaison officer and set him up in a flat in Berlin. He escaped to Switzerland after living it up as a privileged civilian for some months, and was repatriated to Britain, a feat which automatically earned him a Military Cross.*

The *Yubi Maru* stopped to take on oil at Miri, a small refuelling port on the northern tip of Sarawak. The conditions were stifling, but the prisoners were rarely allowed on deck. For much of the time they were forced to remain crouched in the holds with their knees tucked under their chins and their eyes lowered. By this time many of the men were beginning to suffer from severe dehydration, diarrhoea or vomiting. After two-and-a-half days of suffocating heat and stench, the freighter continued its journey through the Balabac Strait at an excruciatingly slow six knots before turning south on the final short run down the east coast of Borneo. Just after sun-up on 18 July, after ten days of oppressive conditions, the *Yubi Maru* finally reached its destination, the small settlement of Sandakan, the peace-time capital of British North Borneo.

---

* While this gives a very human portrait of Jack's nature, the facts are somewhat inaccurate, probably through a mixture of Jack's embellishment and Braithwaite's mis-recalling.

AWM P02326.001

Early days in 'No 1. POW Camp, British North Borneo'

Within 24 hours of landing in Sandakan the Australians were marched from the township to a two-hectare site, which at some time in its past had been a permanent barracks. They had passed a small, recently established police post at the 8 mile peg, continued down rough jungle track through a rubber plantation (part of the pre-war Government Experimental Agriculture Farm), to arrive at a double-barbed wired perimeter fence interspersed with several elevated sentry boxes. On the gate in large, white-painted letters hung the ominous sign, 'No. 1 POW Camp British North Borneo'.

Inside the perimeter, parallel to the front fence and on either side of the gate, were three rows of thatched wooden huts mounted on square-shaped timber stilts. At right angles and to the rear of these buildings were a further 24 closely spaced palm leaf, or *atap*, huts on stilts which appeared to the men to have been more recent additions. Nearby was a huge *mengarris* tree, reaching nearly 70 metres into the air and with enormous buttressed roots, a remnant of the lush rain-forest that had once covered the area. This tree became known as the 'Big Tree', and was a distinctive and symbolic landmark for the men. On the one hand, it was to become a site for many of the hellish parades and tortures carried out by the Japanese, but on the other it was an important symbol of the continuity, strength and endurance that would be needed to sustain these men in the next three years.

The front huts, divided into three distinct rooms and constructed of hardwood planks, housed 64 men each, although this varied, according to the seniority of the men. Each room in the *atap* huts,

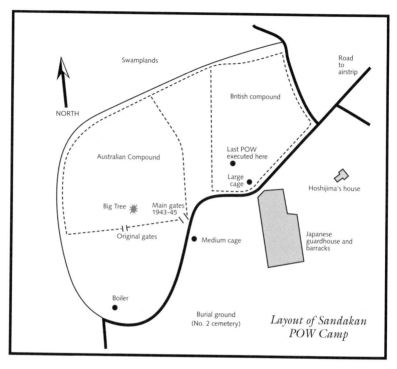

Layout of Sandakan POW Camp

while separated internally with waist-high timber railings, opened out onto a common verandah. There were no doors, a single light bulb dangled from a truss in the centre of the room, and ablution facilities, which were either at the end of or underneath the huts, consisted of large tubs and native-style dippers or a couple of shower heads. Raised platforms of wooden planks ran across the rooms and provided the most cramped of sleeping space, but as Silver describes graphically in her book, these planks had become home to myriad blood-sucking bed bugs, lice and other parasites, a legacy of the huts' former tenants.

On three sides of the camp was vegetation; coffee bushes, occasional patches of tapioca bushes, rubber trees and nondescript scrub. Beyond was the virtually unexplored interior – mountains covered by impenetrable jungle, untamed rivers – populated with small, isolated pockets of tribespeople, most untouched by Western civilisation. The

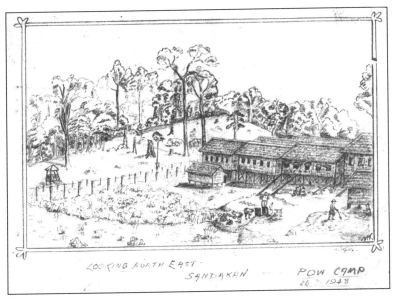

A sketch of Sandakan POW camp, looking north-east.
By Norman McKay Tully (died Ranau, 1/7/1945).

land immediately to the north, however, was generally clear of large trees and, herein lay the purpose for which the Japanese had brought 'B' Force to Sandakan. These prisoners were to construct 3.5 kilometres of road, and from this inhospitable landscape of porous, white, volcanic rock, covered with tangles of scrub, carve out an airstrip for the Japanese war effort.

The airstrip was the idea of an ambitious young lieutenant attached to Japanese headquarters in Borneo. Lieutenant Yamada planned the airstrip to serve as an intermediate refuelling stop for Japanese aircraft flying from Singapore to distant parts of the Philippines and the Dutch East Indies. Despite it being a breach of Geneva conventions to use forced labour for military purposes, he supervised the transport of the prisoners from Singapore to Sandakan. A month after reaching the camp the prisoners were finally informed why the Japanese had brought them to Sandakan. The camp commandant, Captain Hoshijima, assembled the prisoners beneath the

Big Tree, and to the Australians' utter disbelief informed them that they were there to construct an airstrip. 'I have the power of life and death over you,' he told them. 'You will build this aerodrome, if you stay here until your bones rot under the Borneo sun.'

Notwithstanding this, the initial few months of the camp were described by Keith Botterill, one of the Sandakan escapees, as being, under the circumstances, 'as good as you could expect' (*Return to Sandakan*, ABC 1997). The conditions were bearable, the Japanese were not well organised, and the camp was yet to be made escape-proof. In fact quite a number of sorties were carried out at night by the prisoners outside the camp to scavenge or steal food to complement their rations, and at the same time make useful contacts with the local civilian intelligence network, which had been developing since the Japanese occupied Borneo at the beginning of 1942.

Work groups for the airstrip, the construction of the roads, wood gathering and rice collection were also organised. Rod Wells was in charge of the wood gathering group, its purpose being to maintain the boiler which generated the electricity for the camp while at the same time sterilising the drinking water. It was here that Wells met Jack for the first time. Their friendship was initially sparked by the recognition that not only had Wells's father and Jack both served in the First World War, but that they had mutual friends in the Military and Naval Club in Melbourne. The friendship grew by degrees and continued for nearly 12 months before Wells was arrested by the Kempei-tai in July 1943 for secretly building a radio transmitter in the camp. He was sent for trial in Kuching. Wells describes sitting on the verandah of their hut talking about family, children, home, the farm, and not unexpectedly, ways to escape. In one of his letters to Jack's wife at the end of the war Wells writes of how he managed to scavenge some fish using his outside contacts when Jack was confined to hospital, and how Jack was able to return the favour when Wells himself later became ill.

In his second letter to the family, Rod Wells relates:

> I used to sometimes steal bananas and tapioca from the Japs or natives, and John and I would cook it when I got home. He went to the camp hospital in March or early April [1943] with

dysentery. However, after a few weeks he was right and up again. He was thin but in good spirits …

In the early months of the camp work on the airstrip progressed slowly, with the working parties toiling six days a week clearing the growth and moving the topsoil in woven baskets to level the ground. Progress was not helped by the way in which tools were mysteriously 'lost'. Even the addition of rails and handcarts, and a wondrous, steam-driven steamroller, did little to improve the pace. The Australians were ingenious in the creative methods they used to sabotage progress and slow the construction of the airstrip.

However, in October a dramatic change took place. Major Suga, the self-proclaimed commandant of all prisoners of war in Borneo, arrived with due ceremony in Sandakan and assembled the POWs for a special address beneath the Big Tree. He informed them in broken English that work on the strip was progressing too slowly. Not only was the work rate to be lifted and the discipline tightened, but the length of the strip was to be increased and the first stage was to be finished by no later than the end of December, before the monsoonal rains.

To demonstrate his seriousness, Formosan conscripts were brought to the camp to work alongside the Japanese guards, beginning a period of continuous bashings and punishments. Formosa (now Taiwan) was a colony of Japan at the time, and the conscripts brought in to serve in the Japanese army were detested by the Japanese. The Formosans were treated as second-class citizens, so they in turn took out their resentment on the Australian prisoners. From the beginning the prisoners had been subjected to beatings and lashings by the Japanese guards for almost any excuse. With the arrival of the Formosans this regime escalated. Four-man 'basher' gangs roved the airstrip and at any sign of slacking, real or imagined, weighed in with their pick handles, beating the prisoners mercilessly across their backs, heads and shoulders, or on their legs The Formosans also instituted 'group beatings', an accepted part of Japanese army training where soldiers were expected to beat each other while the officers ensured that no one held back. With the Australians, the Formosans added their own hefty and indiscriminate blows to ensure that POWs did not slacken in their delivery.

'Flying practice', punishment for workers on the airstrip.
Drawn by Bill Young.

Another favourite punishment introduced by the Formosans became known as 'flying practice'. Prisoners were forced to stand, sometimes for hours, looking into the sun, with their outstretched arms weighed down by their chonkels (hoes) held in each hand. The first sign of any lowering of the arms was met with a severe beating across the head and shoulders.

With this tightening of camp discipline Hoshijima introduced wooden punishment cages. Keith Botterill (*7.30 Special Report*, ABC 1995), another survivor of Sandakan, described spending nearly 40 days in one of these cages. About 1.3 metres wide and about 1 metre high, the cage was built of narrow wooden slats, set on stilts, and sat outside the main guardhouse next to the Big Tree. Known as 'Esau' by the Japanese, the cage's ceiling was so low that it was impossible for a man to stand up. Later, in mid-1944, a larger cage accommodating up to 17 men was constructed. Botterill describes how for the first three days in the cage he received neither food nor water; after that the rice ration issued every second day was barely sufficient to sustain life. There was no bedding and turns had to be taken to lie down at night because it was impossible for everyone to do so at the same time. Physical jerks were demanded by the guards each day, and any slackening of effort by the prisoners was met with such severe

'Esau', the punishment cage. Drawn by Bill Young.

bashings, Silver reports, that the men were frequently moved to tears by the cruelty.

Not surprisingly, towards the end of 1942 a marked deterioration was beginning to show in the health of the Sandakan POWs. Although there were few deaths at this stage (mainly from dysentery), the POWs were now forced to work every day. There was a noticeable increase in dysentery, malaria, beri-beri and tropical ulcers, some of the latter so advanced that bone showed through. It can reasonably be surmised that it was around this time that Jack Probert spent some time in hospital, as described in Rod Wells's letter. The reason is not known, but it could have been malaria or problems with wounds sustained during World War 1.

At the end of 1942 the first plane finally landed on the airstrip, with due ceremony, and the Japanese eased off on their demands. The men had refused to allow the Japanese to break them, but 1943 was to bring further deterioration in the health of the prisoners and an increase in the cruelty and recriminations by the Japanese.

Resistance and reprisals

For the Australian prisoners the new year represented a year of increasing deprivation and an escalation in the mindless brutality meted out by the Japanese guards and Formosan 'basher gangs'. In April the camp was swollen by the arrival of close to 800 British prisoners, followed later by another group of 500 Australians known as 'E' Force. By mid-year there were nearly 2,500 POWs in Sandakan. Coupled with 5,000 Javanese 'coolies' and a large number of locals, the Japanese had managed to assemble a very large work force expressly for the purpose of constructing the airstrip. A group of 40 new Formosan conscripts also arrived on site; allowed to do whatever they liked, the merciless beating, bashing and caging of the POWs escalated.

During this year many of the intelligence networks both within and outside the camp were discovered by the Japanese, and brutal reprisals inflicted. From the beginning of the Japanese occupation of the Sandakan township, a small but defiant network of Chinese, Malays and European civilians had assisted the Allies in whatever way they could. They planned for the time when they might be able to assist an Allied landing, and they built local resistance groups to help overthrow the Japanese. They also became useful conduits for intelligence to and from the POWs. Unfortunately, most of these networks met with disaster during 1943.

Firstly, in the south of Borneo an armed uprising led by the Dutch Governor ended brutally in July when the Kempei-tai discovered a cache of arms and a radio. The Governor, his wife and 257 people suspected of being implicated were rounded up, tortured and executed. Later, in mid-September in Pontianak, south-west of Sandakan, another local uprising ended in the brutal torture and killing of 1,500 suspects in a swift reprisal by the Japanese. Then, in October, a band of guerillas based in the Jesselton area near Mt Kinabalu had some initial success in overcoming the Japanese, but when the help they expected would be forthcoming from the Philippines failed to materialise the resistance was quickly broken and the guerillas lost over 1,300, a death toll calculated by the counting of severed heads.

These uprisings, linked to a planned revolt at Sandakan itself, led to brutal repercussions within the camp. Since September of the previous year, a small and effective intelligence group under the leadership of Captain Lionel Matthews had been set up in the camp, and with the help of the civilian network, regular messages and food had been successfully smuggled in and out of the camp. However in mid-July, 1943, as the result of a falling out between two friends, one of whom was a member of the civilian underground, the Kempei-tai rounded up a number of local suspects. Under prolonged torture, information was gleaned about both the planned uprising and the passing of wireless parts into the camp. The Kempei-tai suddenly descended on the camp and carried out an extensive search. Matthews, along with a number of others, was arrested. Two days later, some of the rolled-up news summaries which were ready to be smuggled out of the camp were discovered. Wells was forced to admit to their ownership, and therefore at once became the prime suspect for the ownership of a radio, even though that remained undetected by the Japanese despite an extensive search. Confronted with radio parts that had been obtained under duress from a civilian, Wells decided to sacrifice the transmitter and save the receiver. He was arrested and taken to Kempei-tai headquarters.

Silver has graphically described the solitary confinement and brutal interrogation to which Wells was subjected after his arrest. When flogging, beating and conventional torture proved unsuccessful, the torture specialists resorted to more barbaric methods. Wells was rapped repeatedly on the head with a hammer and a bamboo skewer was driven into his ear canal. Refusing to confess, he was then forced to eat cups of rice and drink large quantities of water; as the rice swelled, his stomach and intestines became so distended that the loops of his lower bowel began to protrude from his body. In a final attempt to prise a confession from Wells the Japanese resorted to a brutal and horrifying oriental version of the rack:

> Wells, handcuffed, was suspended by his wrists from one of the verandah rafters so that his knees were about 15 centimetres above the floor. A long plank of wood, about 10 centimetres square, was then placed behind his knees. Two men stood on either side of the plank and the upper body was effectively racked. When the plank was placed across his knees, the flesh was torn from Wells' ankles, causing him to pass out. He called for his mother in his delirium, but never once did he tell his tormentors what they wanted to know.
> (*Sandakan: A Conspiracy of Silence*, p. 132)

Intent on completely dismantling the suspected intelligence network, the Japanese systematically arrested suspect POWs and civilians and relentlessly brutalised them. By mid-September they were able to claim that they had finally broken the Sandakan conspiracy and obtained 'confessions' from the ringleaders. As a result they shipped 52 civilians and 20 POWs, including Wells and Matthews, to Kuching to stand trial for their lives. The men were tied on deck throughout the whole eight-day voyage and had no cover from the sun, rain and waves that washed over the deck.

In his submission to the War Crimes Trials in Tokyo in 1946 Wells describes the court martial and how the Japanese failed to provide a defending officer. The prisoners were not even told the charges against them. They had been compelled to sign or thumbprint statements in Japanese. These had not been translated before they were signed, and the accused did not know what was in them. No evidence was given and they were merely questioned on the statements. The trial was over within half-an-hour. While the others were sentenced to various terms of imprisonment, Matthews's and Wells's names were telegraphed to Tokyo for confirmation of the execution. Unbelievably, in the reply to the request a lowly Japanese telegraphist made a simple error. Instead of recording the number 2 indicating that both were to die he mistakenly tapped out the number 1. As Matthews was the senior in rank he was executed by firing squad while Wells was transferred to Outram Road Gaol in Singapore to serve a prison term of twelve years. He spent two-and-half years in a cell measuring 3 metres by 1 metre before his eventual release by the Allies at the end of 1945.

Meanwhile, as Hoshijima struggled to deal with the conspiracy he became increasingly frustrated. As a consequence bashings increased, food rations were severely cut, and to weaken the camp leadership and morale, in October the Japanese commandant suddenly transferred a number of the Australian officers to Kuching.

During this time the only news of Jack was a postcard sent to his family in May 1943. It consisted of a series of pre-printed standard phrases, parts of which were struck out by Japanese scribes. Jack's only input, apart from indicating what was to be struck out or added, was to sign his name at the bottom of the card. This card was not received by the family until 8 September 1944, sixteen months after its dispatch. In the three years of internment only three messages from Jack in Sandakan were received by the family.

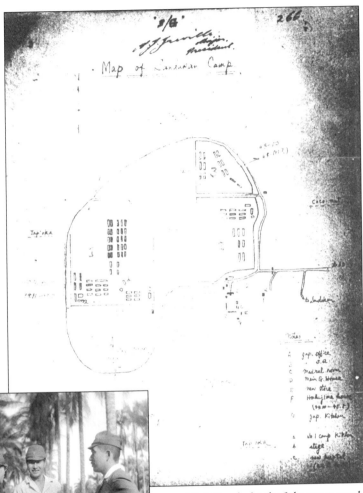

Hoshijima's sketch of the camp, made prior to his trial. (Courtesy Lynette Silver)

Hoshijima (centre) chats with his defence lawyers just before the War Crimes trials commenced. He was tried in Labuan in January 1946, and on 6 April 1946 hanged at Rabaul.

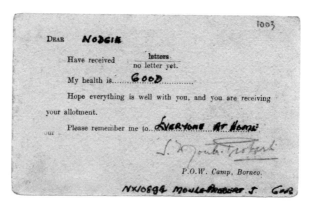

Jack Probert's second postcard home, but the first from Sandakan, written in
May 1943 and received by his family in September 1944.

The time at which the second postcard was dispatched from
Sandakan is unknown – perhaps a some short time after June 1943.
Prefaced with an unusual and formal greeting to his wife, the postcard consisted of two brief typed sentences, a salutation and a signature written in ink. This card was not to reach his family until the end
of the war.

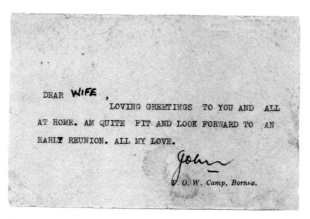

The second message from Sandakan, some time after June, 1943.

Probably shortly after this post card was written, a third and final card representing his last message to his family was despatched.

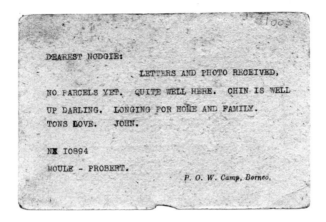

The last message from Sandakan.

Sandakan 1944 – all downhill

The war in the Pacific began to turn for the Allies during late 1943 and early 1944, and the Japanese experienced increasingly severe setbacks as their sea lanes were cut and supplies dislocated. A serious consequence for the Sandakan prisoners was the ever-diminishing supply of rice. It finally ceased in January 1945 and was replaced by tapioca, an indigenous root poor in nutritional value, difficult to digest and poisonous if not prepared properly. In the previous July the vegetable supplements had stopped, and the prisoners had no way to combat the rapid increase in malaria, beri-beri, dysentery and malnutrition. These reduced rations – even though the Japanese expected work on the airstrip to continue – affected the prisoners' health, and at the same time the camp conditions steadily deteriorated. Silver notes that supplies of water and electricity to the camp ceased as cables and pipes were removed for the Japanese barracks, forcing the men to boil up buckets of water hauled from the swamp nearby. Ablutions were now carried out in the polluted swamp, and latrine pits had to be dug and then emptied by hand as the buckets previously used had rusted away.

Silver describes the dramatic spread of dysentery and infection, and how in an effort to keep the outbreaks under control wooden syringes were carved and used by the medical orderlies to remove the pus from sores. Dead flesh was cut away or scraped with whatever implements could be found, and when the corrosive copper sulphate solution used to control the infections ran out, sufferers had their ulcers dabbed with hydrochloric acid.

Inevitably, concessions virtually ceased. The Japanese stopped releasing medical supplies, and any Red Cross parcels received were found to have been already ransacked by the Japanese guards.

By the end of 1944 the death rate among the prisoners was rising. In November the death toll in the Australian camp was 18. In December it reached 56, and in January of the following year 65 prisoners died, an increase bought about by the lack of medical supplies to combat rampaging malarial meningitis and beri-beri. Up to this time prisoners who died were buried in graves with metal markers to identify the site, but when the metal ran out prisoners were buried with no identification, other than in a burial register kept by the Australian camp commander.

The only glimmer of relief from the despair and horror of this existence came on Christmas Day 1944 – in the middle of the morning a heavy raid by American B24 bombers took place, and in successive raids over the next few days rendered the airstrip useless.

The ultimate fate

In 1945 the death rate in the Sandakan camp continued to climb rapidly. In the months leading up to May, over 1,000 Australian and British POWs died from chronic illness, severe malnutrition or mistreatment. All efforts to repair the airstrip were abandoned as a result of constant strafing and bombing, and the prisoners were put to work spreading sullage, collecting wood and foraging for tapioca roots. As the fighting approached Borneo the Japanese became increasingly desperate. In anticipation of Allied attacks on the west coast Hoshijima was instructed to move 360 of his troops and a company of machine gunners to Tuaran on the west coast, taking 455 POWs to act as coolie labourers there.

Route of the Japanese death marches from Sandakan to Ranau.

On 28 January, just after Australia Day, the prisoners set out in 9 groups of 50 on the first of the infamous death marches, from which the only survivors were those who managed to escape. Left behind in the camp were those prisoners too weak to be considered. According to camp records, Jack was not on any of the death marches.

The selected route for the first of the death marches to Ranau – a walking distance of 250 kilometres – was through some of the most tortuous and difficult jungle in the world. The track had originally been prepared for the Japanese, who forced two locals and 'Sandshoe' Willie, a man who knew the territory closely, to assist in its routing. Realising that at some time in the future it might be used to assist the Japanese war effort, they made certain that it passed

*Aerial reconnaissance photograph of Sandakan, showing the airstrip disabled,
but before the bombing of the POW camp on 27 May 1945.*

through the most rugged terrain. They could not anticipate that it would be used by hundreds of Australian and British POWs.

The prisoners left Sandakan mostly barefoot and wearing rags. They were forced to carry the rice rations, cooking gear and munitions of the Japanese troops. At first the track was well-defined, but it soon petered out. The prisoners were forced to wade through running streams and knee-deep mud, attacked voraciously by mosquitoes. Short of food, they scavenged for fern leaves, insects and frogs. Within a short time of leaving Sandakan both the soldiers and prisoners discovered that if they lagged behind they would be killed. Those unable to get up in the morning or those who sat at the side of the track because they could go no further were shot by the Japanese. Major Harry Jackson, sent to Borneo in 1946 by the Australian army to find and reward local people who had helped POWs, filmed a small section of the track. In a documentary showing some of the actual footage he admitted that it was 'hard to reconcile that such dreadful things [could ever] take place' (*Return to Sandakan*, ABC 1995). In the three weeks that it took the first group to march to Ranau, a quarter of the 455 died or were shot. The Japanese troops who survived continued to their coastal destination of Tuaran, leaving the surviving prisoners in Ranau and the village of Paginatan in conditions described by Silver as 'so dreadful it defied the scope of human experience' (*Sandakan: A Conspiracy of Silence*, p. 206).

By the end of May, 30 POWs remained alive. By the time those who survived the second death march arrived at Ranau only 6 were left. By 25 July the sole, emaciated prisoner of the first death march from Sandakan to Ranau had died.

Meanwhile, a severe aerial and naval bombardment of Sandakan by the Allies on 27 May forced the Japanese, expecting an Allied landing, to withdraw to beyond the 11 mile peg. At the same time the POWs fit to assemble beneath the Big Tree were told that they were going to be moved. Because of their condition many were unable to even begin the march. On 29 May, 536 POWs in 11 separate groups left the camp on what was to become the second of the Japanese death marches. They left behind 288 prisoners in the camp.

With the departure of the second death march the Sandakan camp was torched by the Japanese. The Big Tree that had towered over the camp remained.

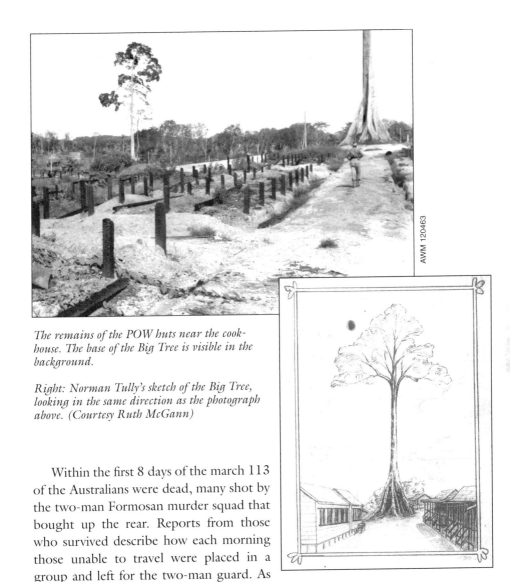

AWM 120463

The remains of the POW huts near the cook-house. The base of the Big Tree is visible in the background.

Right: Norman Tully's sketch of the Big Tree, looking in the same direction as the photograph above. (Courtesy Ruth McGann)

Within the first 8 days of the march 113 of the Australians were dead, many shot by the two-man Formosan murder squad that bought up the rear. Reports from those who survived describe how each morning those unable to travel were placed in a group and left for the two-man guard. As the others continued the march to Ranau they could hear the machine-gun fire that signalled the death of those left behind. On 7 June, a group of 35 POWs were tied by their genitals and massacred at the 55 mile peg. On 26 June, nearly 4 weeks after having left

Sandakan, 183 of the original group arrived at Ranau. The rest had either perished on the track or been diverted to act as 'coolie' labour for the Japanese.

While the second death march was still moving towards Ranau instructions were received by the new Sandakan commandant that all remaining POWs in Sandakan were to be sent to Ranau or disposed of. Seventy-five embarked on this third and final death march, leaving 80 or 90 in the camp, too sick to travel. By the time this group reached the 42 mile peg all were dead.

Meanwhile the POWs from the first and second marches found themselves in the most horrific conditions, and the struggle to remain alive became too great. By 1 August, 32 were still alive. The Japanese guards then dragged 17 of the sickest to a grave site and shot them. On 27 August, 10 more soldiers were led into the jungle and shot. The last five, all officers, were also taken into the jungle, told to sit down, and then shot. Apart from six POWs who managed to escape during the second march or from Ranau and survived to return to Australia, a total of 1,047 Australians and British prisoners perished on these marches.

At the beginning of July, back in Sandakan itself 80 to 90 POWs were still alive. By the end of the second week, 48 remained alive, although close to death. On 13 July 23 POWs were marched down the road to the airstrip and shot. By 15 August, the day Emperor Hirohito surrendered to the Allies, only John Skinner remained alive. He was taken outside the compound, and the last surviving Sandakan POW was decapitated by Murozumi, a Japanese NCO. The same day, Murozumi ordered the destruction of all POW effects, set fire to the barracks and abandoned the camp. When the first of the Allies finally arrived at the 8 Mile Camp two months later on 17 October, all they found was a derelict and overgrown compound, a stark and horrific memorial to the death and degradation of 2,428 Australian and British men by the Japanese in North Borneo.

As prisoners died they were usually wrapped in banana leaves for a short while, and placed with other recent dead under one of the elevated huts. When there were sufficient numbers to warrant raising a burial detail (the remaining POWs were very weak), they were taken

The following represents the content of the telegram shown:

> T.G. 42 Y.
>
> COMMONWEALTH OF AUSTRALIA—POSTMASTER-GENERAL'S DEPARTMENT
>
> **TELEGRAM**
>
> THIS TELEGRAM HAS BEEN RECEIVED SUBJECT TO THE POST AND TELEGRAPH ACT AND REGULATIONS. THE TIME RECEIVED AT THIS OFFICE IS SHOWN AT THE END OF THE MESSAGE.
>
> THE DATE STAMP INDICATES THE DATE OF RECEPTION AND LODGMENT ALSO, UNLESS AN EARLIER DATE IS SHOWN AFTER THE TIME OF LODGMENT.
>
> Office Date Stamp
>
> Office of Origin | No. of Words | Time of Lodgment
>
> ARMY RECORDS VIA SYDNEY 59/1 4P
>
> POSTAL ACKNOWLEDGEMENT BELY PERSONAL DELIVERY
> MRS NORA MOULEPROBERT
> BOX 81 GRIFFITH NSW
>
> IT IS WITH DEEP REGRET THAT I HAVE TO INFORM YOU THAT NX10894 GUNNER JOHN MOULEPROBERT DIED WHILST PRISONER OF WAR SANDAKAN BORNEO ON 10 MAY 1945 AND DESIRE TO CONVEY TO YOU THE PROFOUND SYMPATHY OF THE MINISTER FOR THE ARMY MINISTER FOR THE ARMY
>
> 4 3op@

The telegram received by Nora Probert on 31 October 1945. Jack's final postcard from Sandakan (see page 169) arrived after the telegram.

and buried in the Number 2 cemetery, just outside the perimeter of the camp and close to the boiler.

Due to the shortage of wood, most of the burials were carried out using coffins with false bottoms so they could be recycled. It is possible that a short service was said over the graves by either Padre Thompson or Padre Greenwood. At first wrapped in blankets, and when these ran out banana leaves, bodies were placed in individual graves and the site and name systematically recorded in a log kept by the Australian camp commander. This crucial record – which the prisoners had agreed must at all costs survive the camp – was inevitably lost. Therefore, despite being buried in single graves, very few of these men were able to be identified when they were later located and disinterred.

When the Australian War Graves recovery unit arrived in North Borneo in 1945 and disinterred the bodies of the POWs, they transferred them over the following eighteen months to what ultimately became only a holding cemetery, sited on the infamous airstrip just north of the camp.

The site proved to be unsuitable due to the high water table, and

An Australian War Graves unit inspects the graves at Sandakan No. 2 cemetery in 1945.

in 1947 the graves unit buried the men for a third and final time, on the small island of Labuan just off the northern coast of present-day Sabah. This is where Jack Probert presumably now lies, among 345 graves still unidentified in the Australian War Cemetery.

Jack's actual fate will never be precisely known. But according to Japanese records only recently made accessible, Jack became sick with malaria in early April 1945 and died on 10 May 1945.

Just three months later, in August, the Japanese surrendered.

Epilogue

We had always harboured vague feelings that some day we would visit Borneo and the infamous prison site where our father had spent his final days. However it was not until the discovery of Rod Wells's letter and the search that followed that feelings began to crystallise into something more compelling. With the end of Jack's story in sight we felt we were finally ready to make the step and visit Borneo.

As it turned out, the impetus for this final step in our journey came from Lynette Silver, who from the time we had first contacted her in 1998 had provided us with continuous support and encouragement. At a couple of critical times her experience in tracking down difficult and elusive sources had proved of inestimable value in closing gaps in our evolving story. She invited us to join her and a small group of relatives to visit Borneo in late August 1999.

We met up with the group in Singapore, as it was here that the story of Sandakan had really begun. On 15 February in 1942 the Australians had been captured by the Japanese. Before being sent to Sandakan they had either been sent out on working parties or interned in the Selarang Barracks for five, long uncertain months. Most of the tour group we were meeting had lost men either in Sandakan or on the death march route to Ranau. They had joined the group to see the infamous places their men had experienced, and to put substance, in some small way, to what for them had been merely names on a map for almost sixty years.

Jan Welsh (daughter of Bob Downey) had made the long trip from northern NSW to find the place along the Sandakan to Ranau track where her father had died on the first of the Japanese marches in early 1945. Brian Hales's uncle had died in Ranau in 1945. There was Graham Sandercock, now in his late fifties, whose father had managed to survive in Sandakan until April of 1945, as had Harry Toms, uncle of Warren Brampton. Audrey Buckley and Elsie Clark lost their brother in the Sandakan camp in the same month that Jack had died. Harry Pallister, accompanied by his fourteen-year-old grandson, Dan, wished to commemorate his father at the 44 mile peg, near where he had perished on the second death march to Ranau, and to see his grave, one of 18 recently identified by Lynette in Labuan Cemetery.

That first day in Singapore was strangely satisfying. The circumstances of the original capture of the Australians began to take on a deeper meaning as we visited significant sites and relived a little of the final days of the island before its surrender to the Commander of the Japanese forces, General Yamashita. At Fort Canning Hill we viewed the Headquarters and Malay Command Post of General Percival, created by the British for the defence of Malaya and Singapore. Here we observed a dramatic reconstruction of the surrender decision made by the British Officers, conveyed cleverly by audio and visual effects, animatronics and crafted figurines. We visited Mount Faber, known before the War as Fort Faber, where at the time of the Japanese advance down the Malay peninsula the huge 14 inch guns faced seaward to protect Singapore from attack. We visited the Kranji War Cemetery on the northern coast of Singapore, close to where the first wave of Japanese troops landed in early February of 1942. We paused briefly to view the Causeway, which was partly blown up by the retreating British troops on the last day of January in 1942, and where Jack was said to have been sighted handing out toddies of rum to some of the retreating troops.

We also traced the route of the POWs after the surrender, from the Esplanade to the Selarang Barracks on the Changi peninsula. We drove past the Alexandra Military Hospital where advancing Japanese troops had massacred Indian troops, surgeons and the wounded who were in the hospital at the time. We passed along Clementi Road to the location of the original Bukit Timah village, the site of one of the fiercest battles of the Singapore campaign, and where, it is said, Jack as a POW had 'borrowed' the post office clock and stuffed it in his kitbag.

The following day, we flew to Sandakan, now the second largest city in the modern East Malaysian state of Sabah. It was a hot, humid afternoon. Grey rain clouds had begun their inevitable afternoon entry from the west and the suffocating equatorial heat buffeted us as we made our way across the tarmac to the terminal. For quite some time before landing we had flown over miles of tropical jungle, interrupted only by long, winding, silt-brown rivers and an occasional, isolated village settlement. As we neared Sandakan the village settlements had grown in number and equatorial jungle had begun to give way to expansive estates of palm oil.

No sooner had we landed at the Sandakan airport than we were confronted with our first evidence of the POW experience. A little distance to the left of the terminal and running north across the horizon we could just make out slightly raised ridges of volcanic rock. To the everyday traveller these would have been unremarkable, but to us the ridges represented the outer extremities of the area that the Sandakan prisoners had been forced to level by hand, and over a period of three years turn into an airstrip for the Japanese. Here, in front of us, was the very reason the POWs were sent to Borneo.

From the compact, modern airport a bus took us to the city. Our hotel sat a few streets back from the busy Sandakan waterfront, with an expansive view of one of the largest land-locked harbours in the world. From our hotel window we faced the shimmering expanse of the harbour, and at its northern extremity we could make out the clear, black line of Berhala Island, where in 1943 'E' Force had spent two months before joining the Australians at Sandakan. It was not too difficult to conjure up in our mind's eye an image of the fateful *Yubi Maru* as it steamed across the top of this horizon that hot July morning back in July 1942 with its 1,500 Australian POWs, and tied up alongside a wharf that we could just make out, immediately below us, through a break between the high rise buildings. Unlike today's noisy, populous and sprawling city, dawn of that morning would have revealed to the few Australians fortunate enough to be allowed on deck a small British colonial township with cluttered streets of low, single-storeyed, red-roofed buildings.

For both of us it was a strange and confusing feeling to be now actually in Sandakan. For so long this name had lain dormant at the back of our minds, yet it had paradoxically been central to our lives. For few other Australians would it have held much relevance. An obscure place on the map. Of little meaning. Yet we had lived with this name like people live with the name of the place in which they had been born. Our earliest memories had always harboured this name. It had represented feelings and vague imaginings that were about to be tested for the first time.

Late on that first afternoon in Sandakan we joined our bus and made our way past the old wharf through narrow, winding, harbour-side streets to the town's main sports field with its small concrete grandstand and open stalls. As we walked onto the grass of the playing field a few of the locals watched inquisitively. It was here that some of the men from 'B' Force camped on their first night in Borneo, a staging post between the wharf and their destination, the POW camp. That afternoon they had disembarked unsteadily down the gangplank, had their legs sprayed with carbolic acid and under escort of their Japanese guards been brought to this open, grassy space, the *padang*, just a short distance west of the township.

We then took the bus through winding streets to the church of St Michael and All Angels, just a short distance further on. It was a bright, warm sunny Saturday afternoon and as we alighted loud music could be heard from inside the church. Local people were going about their tasks preparing for the following morning's services. At first Sherriff remained outside walking the gardens, but John slipped inside the building and quietly slid into a pew at the back of the church. He sat unobtrusively in the shadows musing, and half watching a group of teenage girls in the sanctuary, obviously rehearsing a dance routine to the music. He was not at all sure why a visit to the church had been included; for some reason he had missed the earlier explanation. As he sat, he experienced a cold, strange, prickly feeling creeping through him. An inexplicable wave of sadness suddenly swept over him and he felt tears welling up in his eyes. Seeing him quietly sitting by himself Lynette slipped in and joined him. It took him a few moments to regain his composure and ask the reason for the visit to the church. Quietly he was told how the fittest members of 'B' Force had been housed right here, in this church, on that first night in Sandakan. Some had remained on the boat. Some had slept in the open on the *padang*, but the fittest

The church of St Michael and All Angels. Lynette Silver is standing in front.

of the prisoners, after an evening meal of limed rice washed down with watery tea, had been marched by the Japanese up the winding road to St Michael's and that night had slept here, on the concrete floor of the church. At that moment John thought that he understood his feelings. Jack had been right here – not just in Sandakan but in this small, stone church. He felt that suddenly he had crossed his father's path for the first time in fifty-eight years.

Early the next morning our party embarked on what was to be one of the most emotionally trying parts of our trip, a return to the site of the original Sandakan POW camp. We left early and joined the normal busy morning traffic along the same road that the Australian prisoners had trudged in their march to the camp. We turned right at the site of the old Eight Mile Post and followed what had been the track to the camp, until the bus drew up at the entrance to the Sandakan Memorial Park.

Today, most of the prison compounds and the site of the Japanese barracks have become general housing and sprawling industrial development. The current park, established by the Australian Government in 1995, incorporates all that remains of the original POW site: the camp's boiler, its water tanks and a small section of the former No. 1 Camp.

We wandered through the park for the most part lost in our own thoughts. We could hear the sounds of the traffic beyond the park and the noise of jackhammers working somewhere on the industrial and building sites to the north. We found the site of the original entrance to the camp and the Japanese guard-house. We paused at the rusted remains of the boiler that had supplied the electricity to the camp through the efforts of the wood party, of which both Jack Probert and Rod Wells had been members. We saw the remains of the Ruston-Bucyrus excavator with its wheels encased in concrete, a small monument to the prisoners' creative sabotage to prevent its use in levelling the airstrip. We located the approximate sites of the *atap* huts of the Australian POWs, the 'Big Tree', and the cages in which many of the prisoners had suffered brutal punishment. We moved quietly through the small Interpretation Centre, absorbing the drawings, photographs and text portraying the excoriating story of the camp and its men. We walked the pathways edged with hibiscus and sprawling native bushes, trying to reconcile the peace and serenity of the surroundings with the deprivation and savagery that had been experienced there.

As our time at the park drew to a close we finally gathered at the memorial, a stark, grey, highly polished slab of Australian granite set inside the original boundary of the camp and adjacent to the site of the infamous Big Tree. Surrounded by the tall, straight trunks of remnant rainforest trees, and overlooking the park, the group held a short and touching service commemorating the men who had perished within these confines. We laid wreathes, burned gum leaves, and John left on the steps of the memorial a small bunch of wattle he had brought all the way from home. It was a short, simple ceremony that moved many to tears.

Our journey from Sandakan to Ranau took only a few hours. In contrast, the 455 men in the first death march in 1945 had taken from 28 January to the middle of February before the first of its survivors staggered into Ranau. The track they followed had made its

Sherriff and John at the Sandakan memorial (right). Below, the remains of the boiler at the camp.

way through the jungle, away from the present-day highway. In places the highway runs south of the track, in other places north, before the two converge at the village of Paginatan. Today, much of the dense jungle, particularly from Sandakan to Telupid, has been cleared and replaced with vast estates of oil palms. Alongside the busy highway, at a spot close to the place where Bob Pallister had perished, the group stopped and held a brief, informal service to commemorate his death. Just a little further on, at the 52 mile peg we paused again, this time to commemorate where Bob Downey had died.

Then, following the sealed road from the village of Paginatan, we moved out of the heavy jungle and climbed into highlands. The road narrowed and grew more tight and circuitous. Worrying drops fell away from the road into valleys as we continued to climb. Small

SERVICE AND CASUALTY FORM

2 Rfts. 2/15 Fld. Regt

A.F. B.103—1 (Adapted)
Army No. NX 10894

Unit 1st Fld Tng Regt

Rank GNR (On Enlistment)	Christian Names John	Surname MOULE - PROBERT (Block Capitals)

Date of Enlistment 20-5-41 (MOB 2 No. 8544)
Place Paddington N.S.W.
Date of Birth 15-11-01
Place of Birth Victoria Melbourne
Trade or Occupation Produce Merchant
Religion C of E

Medical Classification—Class I. (On Enlistment)

Marital Condition Married Box 81 Griffith N.S.W.
Next of Kin Nora Moule Probert
Address of Next of Kin ~~Box~~ Hemi H.C. Dansford Griffith NSW KING & CASTLEREAGH STS SYDNEY
Relationship Wife

Identification—Colour of Hair fair Eyes blue
Distinctive Marks Linear Scar Rt Upper Arm

Date	From whom received	Record of all casualties regarding promotions (acting, temporary, local or substantive), appointments, transfers, postings, attachments, &c., forfeiture of pay, wounds, accidents, admission to and discharge from Hospital, Casualty Clearing Stations &c. Date of disembarkation and embarkation from a theatre of war (including furlough, &c.).	Date of Casualty	Place of Casualty	Authority W.3011, B.2069, or other Document	Signature of Officer Certifying Correctness of Entries
21-5-41	G.D.D.	Marched in to G.D.D	20-5-41	Sydney	W30 11	74
22-5-41	"	Marched out to 1 Fld Trng Regt	21-5-41	"		247
22-5-41	C/O 1 Fld Trg	Taken on strength ex O.D.D.	20-5-41	Cowra	W3011 809/141 Ln
29-5-41	"	N/K address now c/o H.C. Dansford Bank N.S.W. King	15-5-41	"	W3011 Tm
6-8-41	2/15	Embarked for I.I.	29-7-41	Sydney	Rob. 53-5-64 uN.
30-8-41	2/15 F.K.	Disembarked Singapore	16-8-41	Abroad	2/147 85
27-9-41	"	T.O.S. + Rfts	24-9-41	"	7/428 83
4-10-41	"	Adm 10 A.G.H. mumps and posted to x list	30-9-41	"	8/488
25-10-41	"	Tsfd to 2 C.D. x 10 A.G.H. (enfect Parotitis)	20-10-41	"	11/344 CRS
15-11-41	"	Mobile + T.O.S. + Reinf 2/15 Fld Regt G.B.D.	14-11-41	"	14/1672 CRS
					102	

Date	From whom received	Record of all casualties regarding promotions (acting, temporary, local or substantive), appointments, transfers, postings, attachments, &c., forfeiture of pay, wounds, accidents, admission to and discharge from Hospital, Casualty Clearing Stations &c. Date of disembarkation and embarkation from a theatre of war (including furlough, &c.).	Date of Casualty	Place of Casualty	Authority W.3011, B.2069, or other Document	Signature of Officer Certifying Correctness of Entries
		NX 10894 Moule Probert J				
24-11-41	AIF G.B.D.	Taken ex 2 Con Dep and struck of x list 2/15 Fld Regt	31-10-41	Abroad	11/144 290	
2-12-41	"	M/out to 2/15 Fld Regt	14-11-41	"	24/7143 188	
		2 M.D. RECORDS OFFICE				
9 APR 1943	AIF Malaya	MISSING. PRISONER of WAR - Borneo	16-2-42	Malaya	8/189 20/32	RD
		NSW Echelon and Records				
2010/45	MI PW P/A	DEC'D WHILST P.O.W. same r/s N8	10-5-45	Sandakan	CAS 2073 NX/246/45 9456 17/43/9716	
4-4-45	NSW Life	N/K CQA Box 81 Griffith	31-3-45	NSW	17/35/1311	
		GRATUITY CHECKED - 7 JAN 1946				
		RECONCILED 29 MAY 1946				

A.H.M.—3/41—B461

The cairn at Ranau consists of one stone for each man who died on the marches.

villages and settlements could be seen off in the distant valleys, and then, quite unexpectedly, we caught glimpses of a jagged, black peak slipping in and out of the cloud cover. Gradually it revealed itself as a mountain, angular and foreboding. This was for the Ranau prisoners the infamous Mt Kinabalu; the craggy, granite sentinel overlooking the village of Ranau. Apart from three Australian prisoners who successfully escaped from here in July 1945, all those who finally reached this place perished. It is almost as if Kinabalu now stands as a monument overlooking the final resting places of those Sandakan prisoners.

When the survivors of the first death march arrived in Ranau in mid February 1945 they were in such a weakened state that the Japanese had been unable to force them to travel further. So they left the prisoners in the hands of the local Japanese Area Commander and the battalion had pressed on to the coast. The men were put to work around the camp and the fittest were placed on the infamous rice-carrying parties, lumping 20 kilogram bags on their backs for the prisoners and Japanese soldiers still at or passing through Paginatan.

Today nothing remains of the three camps that once held the Australian and British prisoners at Ranau. However, at the site of the original No. 1 Camp, on the northern bank of a boulder-strewn river and now in the grounds of a local church, the Australian Returned Services League has erected a simple cairn of river stones as a memorial, each stone representing a prisoner who died at Ranau.

We stood quietly in the shade of the large tree next to this cairn, and could see the ring of low hills stretching away into the middle distance with a horizon of high rainforest country just beyond.

We could imagine how the prisoners must have wondered at the inhumanity of their existence as they looked across this wide upland valley and saw small farming plots spread out along the river flats, water buffalo working in the fields, and villagers peacefully cultivating their rice and vegetables. It was impossible to reconcile the tranquility of the place with the brutality and deprivation that the men of Ranau had endured.

At this place none would have met a worse fate than that of Gunner Cleary, who in March 1945 had lain chained to the tree close to where we now stood. Along with a mate, he had attempted to escape. He was recaptured and subjected to horrendous treatment at the hands of the Japanese. For four days he was tied by his neck to the tree outside the guardhouse, covered in blood and bruises and dirtied by dysentery. His condition had rapidly deteriorated and mates wept, unable to do anything to relieve his humiliation. Eight days later he was finally released by his tormentors, who dumped him alongside the track. By the time his friends could finally attend to him Cleary was near death. At the creek they tenderly washed him, before carrying him back to the hut where he died in the arms of his mates.

Our group gathered around the simple cairn. Lynette Silver spoke movingly of the significance of the site. A poem written by Bill Young, one of the survivors of Sandakan, was read by Jan Welsh, while Brian Hales, whose uncle had died here in April 1945, read verses from the Gospel of St John. Hymns were sung, wreathes laid, and a minute's silence observed. And then we carried out a ritual that now began to mark each of the significant stops on our trip, the burning of Australian gum leaves in a small clay bowl at the base of the memorial. As the distinctive grey, pungent smoke curled away into the highlands air we each stood quietly, lost in our thoughts of that distant time.

The next day we travelled the final leg down through mountainous country towards the coast to Sabah's major city, Kota Kinabalu, known at the time of the Japanese occupation as Jesselton. For most of the journey to this point our energies had been focussed on the tragedy of Sandakan and the fate of the Australian and British prisoners in Borneo. But the occupation of Borneo by the Japanese also had frightful consequences for its local and indigenous population, and probably none more so than those who had lived in Jesselton in October 1943.

At the time, a force of young Chinese men, local Dusan farmers, islanders, Murut tribesmen from the interior, with members of the then recently disbanded North Borneo volunteers, carried out a major local uprising against the Japanese. With assistance from a Philippines guerilla force, their plan had been to capture Jesselton and some of its nearby centres from the Japanese and hold them until the Allies could mount an invasion force to drive the Japanese from Borneo. The force experienced initial success and Jesselton and some of the centres were quickly captured by the guerilla forces, but the assistance expected failed to materialise and within days the Japanese had regrouped. Their reprisals were swift and bloody.

The revolt managed to continue for a further two months, with the guerillas attacking pockets of Japanese stationed at various points along the coast and in the hinterland. However without the promised assistance from their Filippino counterparts, the revolt faltered and the guerillas were forced to surrender. Albert Qwok, the leader of the revolt, and his four lieutenants were beheaded at Petegas and the remainder of his men machine-gunned to death. A further 176 civilians found guilty of assisting the rebels were executed by firing squad, while unknown thousands of locals died at the hands of the Japanese in their subsequent purges. To honour this local disaster we visited the gardens and memorial in Petegas Park dedicated to the thousands, many unknown, who died as a result of this insurrection.

For both of us, one of the highlights of our journey was our meeting with a sprightly eighty-year-old Chinese man called Sini. On our final night in Kota, Lynette had arranged for him to join us at the Raffelesia, a local city restaurant. Sini, whose real name is Chin Chee Kong, had been a prominent member of the Sandakan resistance group. As a slight, nineteen-year-old who spoke good English, he had changed his name and taken a job as a Chinese coolie at the stores office on the airstrip at Sandakan in order to be close to the prisoners. It was difficult for both of us to believe that here was a man who had been involved in the very experiences of Sandakan. Here was a man who had passed on news and information to men from that camp; had perhaps shared a cigarette or passed the time of day with many of them. Fiercely patriotic, he had worked closely with Sandakan's internal camp intelligence organisation and at great peril carried messages, letters and maps between it and the local underground. He had helped smuggle food, medicine and surgical instruments into the camp, and had even carried in some of the chemicals Rod Wells used to construct the camp's radio receiver.

Because of his broad local knowledge, Sini had strongly believed that the most likely escape route for Sandakan escapees was by sea, so he had attempted to co-ordinate ways and means whereby prisoners in small groups might escape through the Chinese underground and across the Sulu Sea to link up with Filippino guerillas. Unfortunately these plans were never realised.

With the unexpected collapse of the camp intelligence group in 1943, this man with whom we now conversed was arrested by the

Labuan Cemetery, with its elegant lawns and simple white stone cross.

Kempei-tai, and along with the other conspirators, interrogated and tortured for days. He had been taken to Kuching for trial and sentenced by the Japanese to four years imprisonment.

For us this evening had been a powerful conduit into the Sandakan of the past.

***

The island of Labuan is a three-hour ferry ride across the South China Sea, south-west of Kota Kinabalu. Three kilometres from Port Victoria, the island's main township, lies the Labuan War Cemetery. Converted in 1946 from a patch of rough jungle, it has become one of the most beautiful war cemeteries in the Pacific islands. Flame trees line its eastern boundary, and bordering its gardens to the south and west are huge, flowering West African tulip trees and majestic palms. Gardenias and red roses flower in borders that divide the burial plots, and hibiscus, oleanders, wild orchids and bright scarlet climbers contrast with the verdant green of the manicured lawns. Neat serried

AWM P02467.072

The official paybook photograph, taken on enlistment,
of NX10894 Gunner John Moule-Probert.

Below: names of Australian and Allied soldiers who perished in Borneo are
recorded on bronze panels at the Labuan cemetery.

NX10554 MILLER A. M.
NX24065 MOTLEY L.
NX10894 MOULE-PROBERT J. MM.
NX19749 MOXHAM H. W.
NX30917 MYERS J. R.

Sherriff (left) and John (above) at the gravestone adopted to honour their father.

rows of bronze plaques on low pedestals mark the graves of Allied soldiers, sailors and airmen. In the centre, overlooking the park, stands an elegant white granite Cross of Sacrifice. This is the final burial place of those who died in Sandakan, Ranau and along the track. Here, somewhere among a group of 345 unidentified graves, is the final burial place of Jack Probert.

This visit to the Labuan cemetery was the final step in our journey. The group was subdued as the bus made its way out of the Port Victoria township and joined the narrow Jalan Tanjong Batu road leading to the cemetery.

Then suddenly we were there. We had reached the memorial gates and brick cloisters that mark the entrance to the Labuan War Cemetery. The journey that began with a letter in an old black valise was finally drawing to a conclusion.

The hours that followed produced the most poignant and deeply felt emotions we experienced throughout the trip. Somewhere in this broad expanse of lawn memorials were the final remains of Jack Probert, our father. We will never know exactly where. His is simply one of the 345 unidentified graves from the Sandakan No. 2 cemetery, engraved with the simple but searingly affective epitaph, 'Known Unto God, An Australian of the 1939–1945 War'.

As the morning drew to a close we decided that we needed to adopt a grave that might represent our father, a place that would at least allow us a focus for this final journey. At the end of one of the rows in the southern section of the park we selected one specific grave. We left small crosses embellished with the details of Jack's life and silently farewelled the man whose life we had only just discovered.

The circle had at last been closed.

APPENDIX 1

Awards for Valour

One of the real mysteries we faced in compiling Jack's story was the conflicting information we discovered about the military honours he won during the First World War.

We know that during the First World War Jack Probert was awarded the Military Medal (MM), as the family possesses the medal with its edge engraved '4821 Pte J.W. Probert 1/RIF.BRIG', together with its dark blue, white and crimson ribbon. We know too, that the publication of the award was not only delayed for a number of years, but when originally published it was accredited to the wrong soldier. We found that on 19 November 1918, just eight days after peace had been declared, the *London Gazette* noted that a Military Medal had been awarded to John William Moule-Hopkins. There was no citation. On 14 January 1920, fourteen months later, the *Gazette* carried a correction pointing out that in fact John William Moule-Probert had been awarded the Military Medal. Again, there was no citation.

We still do not know the manner in which this award was won. A search of both British and Australian military records failed to elicit any pertinent information, although we discovered it was not unusual for an award (particularly a Military Medal) to be made without an accompanying testimony. In the early period of the First World War this lack of a citation frequently resulted from the confusion prevailing on the battlefield. Or it might simply be the result of the death, injury or relocation of the officer responsible for substantiating and writing up the details of such actions. We discovered an additional complication: even when citations were actually compiled soldiers often received the only copy and were simply instructed that they had sole responsibility for its safe-keeping. It is easy to understand how these could be subsequently lost.

In Jack's case, official publication of the award came almost four-and-half years after the original action, after he had changed services, and months after he had been discharged and repatriated to Australia. Further complicating the matter, all Jack's First World War military records, apart from his RFC/RAF records, appear to have been lost during the bombing of London in the Second World War. However, 'Military Medal' is formally recorded alongside his name on all official Australian cenotaphs, in Canberra, Griffith and Sandakan, as well as on the Australian War Cemetery Memorial on Labuan Island.

Without a citation to describe the act for which the medal was awarded we have had to rely on deduction and secondary sources of information. According to Melbourne Grammar School records, (see R.W.E. Wilmot (ed.), *A History of the Church of England Grammar School, Melbourne*; J.B. Kiddle, *War Services of Old Melburnians, 1914–1918*) Jack's MM was won during one the first battles of the war and before he was captured. By carefully tracing the movements of his company, using the daily field diaries of the First Battalion of the Rifle Brigade, we are now convinced that in August 1914 Jack won his MM in an action during the Battle of Le Cateau and just prior to his capture in Ligny Cathedral. He sustained leg and head injuries as a result of the action. The records at the Australian War Memorial support this contention.

There is strong evidence that Jack also won the Military Cross (MC). We know that all British soldiers were automatically awarded an MM (ranks) or an MC (officers) for escape from an enemy POW camp. Jack escaped from Döberitz in Germany in September 1917. We have been unable to locate any gazetting of the award, and can only surmise that the actual escape could not be confirmed until his escape partner Geoffrey Whitlock made it out on a similar route in mid 1918. We have found numerous references in both official and unofficial records to Jack's MC. For example, we know from the ABC interviews with Dick Braithwaite that Jack wore the distinctive purple and white ribbon on a parade in Singapore. During a telling exchange (see p. 147) between a visiting British General and Jack whilst on a parade, Braithwaite records the surprise expressed by the General to find a former British officer, wearing the Military Cross ribbon, standing in the ranks.

Additional support evidence for his winning of the MC can be found in the biographic reference cards compiled in 1919-1920 by C.E.W. Bean, Official Australian War Historian, and used by him in compiling his official histories. Jack's three cards, held at the Australian War Memorial in Canberra, appear to have been consolidated from his First World War army and airforce records, at a time when his records must have been still available to the historian. These cards clearly document and date his winning of both the MM and the MC. They refer to Lieutenant John William Moule Probert MC MM, and note that he was awarded the MC on 3 December 1917.

Internal correspondence between central Army Records and the Pay Officer of Eastern Command in Melbourne reviewing his war gratuity on 23 May 1950 clearly refers to John William Probert MC MM.

Supplementary evidence is contained in the 1920 edition of Melbourne Grammar School's war records, which documents Jack's achievement of an army commission on 3 December 1917 and the award of a Military Cross for escaping from a German POW camp in the same year. (It should be noted that by entering the RFC in December 1917 he would have forgone this army promotion.)

The final element to this mystery is that Jack's dress medals pin bar, which we hold, has a gap on the right hand precedence space immediately ahead of the MM. We have no alternative explanation of why this space, which would normally be taken by a higher award (such as the MC), remains blank.

We have experienced difficulties in assembling and assessing this information. The evidence is scattered and in places open to interpretation. It has been made difficult not only by the loss of crucial records, particularly the British military records, but also by the twists and turns of Jack's war career. During the First World War Jack was an Australian serving in the British Forces. He served in both its army and air force. He was a corporal in the Rifle Brigade gazetted for promotion to Lieutenant after his POW camp escape, but never took up this promotion. He was a flying cadet in the old Royal Flying Corps before he 'won his wings' and became a Second Lieutenant in the newly proclaimed Royal Air Force in 1918. After his father's death in 1917 and prior to entering the RFC he changed his name to include one of his father's Christian names. Sometimes this is recorded as a hyphenated name, at others as an additional Christian name. There is little wonder that records have been lost or become confused.

Nevertheless, despite our inability to uncover official documentation there appears to be sufficient evidence that Jack Probert won both the MC and the MM during the First World War.

Was Jack's Experience Unique?

When we began this investigation we did not know that Jack had been a prisoner of war in both world wars. Discovering this striking coincidence, we began to wonder just how unusual this might be. How many other Australian soldiers like Jack might have become POWs in both of these wars?

It is worth noting the time frame Jack's service encompassed in order to appreciate how few Australians might be in a similar position to Jack. When Jack first went to war in August 1914 he was twenty years old. At war's end he was twenty-five. So when World War 2 broke out a little over twenty years later, Jack was 46 and officially too old to enlist. Coupled with the fact that in World War 1 Australian soldiers were not exposed to capture as early as other Allied contingents (the Gallipoli campaign lasted until September 1915 and there were very few prisoners) and assuming an enlistment age of 18, veterans from World War 1, at a minimum, would have been forty-three at the start of World War 2, at the time an illegal age for enlistment.

During the time of writing we raised the question of the possible uniqueness of Jack's experience with a range of historians and military authorities; however, at the date of publication of this book we have been unable to find a definitive answer. We have discovered that military records are incomplete, personal recollections are too unsure to be reliable, and that, in general, research processes appear to be currently inadequate to resolve such an issue decisively.

For example, when we examined the records we found that some

World War 1 veterans not only changed their age when they enlisted for a second time in 1939, but also their names. Because of this and other such difficulties, we feel the only way we might eventually find a satisfactory answer might be from the public domain of anecdotal stories stimulated by the publication of this book.

What is clear is that, actuarially, only a small number of soldiers at the most could have had Jack's experience. In the World War 1 4,000 Australians fell into enemy hands and while some of these would have re-enlisted in the Second World War, the majority would have been unable to rejoin for reasons of age or infirmity. Many, too, would have died during the period between the wars.

So far there have been one or two possible instances of multiple imprisonments brought to our attention, but as yet military historians have been unable to confirm the details of the case.

(For example, there is anecdotal evidence of an Australian soldier, who was captured in World War 1, captured again briefly by the Vichy French in the Middle East in World War 2, and then captured again by the Japanese! Staff at the Australian War Memorial have been unable to confirm the details of the case.)

We have therefore concluded that Jack Probert's position as a prisoner of both World Wars is very close to unique, though perhaps not unique. At this stage there are no other documented cases.

(We have not investigated possible multiple imprisonments involving other wars such as the Boer, Korea or Vietnam.)

Perhaps this book might bring to light other Australians who were imprisoned in both World Wars.

APPENDIX 3

Time-line & Jack's Family

Grandparents' and Parents' life

31 May 1815	William Richard, Jack's grandfather born Newport, England
8 May 1832	William Richard sails as a midshipman on the *Recovery* to Newfoundland
30 March 1835	Joins East India Company as midshipman
2 June 1851	Receives Master's Certificate
21 April 1853	With wife Elizabeth, William Richard departs Bristol for Melbourne on the *Protector* for a new life in the colonies
August 1853	Arrives in Bendigo gold diggings
30 March 1855	Jack's father, Charles born, Williamstown, Victoria. Charles' mother dies a week later from typhus
28 April 1862	Charles returns to England with his father
29 January 1863	William Richard marries a widow, Lucinda Hunt. Six children born of this marriage
27 January 1871	William Richard and Lucinda divorce
19 August 1873	William Richard returns to Australia with Charles and his two step-brothers. William becomes a pastor for the Plymouth Brethren in Melbourne
1877–1889	Charles works at numerous jobs in Victoria, New South Wales, Northern Queensland and Northern Territory to pay off debts accrued on his return to Australia
7 August 1889	Charles marries Maud Mary Woodward in Bendigo
1889	William Richard returns to live in England

Jack's Life

15 November 1893	Jack born in Elsternwick, Melbourne
1 July 1901	Charles divorces Maud Mary
22 January 1903	William Richard dies at Bevils, aged 87
15 July 1905	Charles marries Elsie May Vanden Hooten
February 1905	Jack enrols at Cumloden, a preparatory school for Melbourne Grammar
February 1906	Jack enrols at Melbourne Grammar
May 1910	Jack appears before Castlemaine Police Court
19 July 1910	Receives six months in Darlinghurst Gaol, Sydney, for false pretences
17 August 1910	Released from Darlinghurst and taken on as a 'boy' on the windjammer *Marian Woodside*
March 1911	Returns from Chile to Sydney
1 May 1911	Receives twelve months in Goulburn Gaol in New South Wales for false pretences
July 1912	Jack sails for England
23 September 1912	Joins the British Rifle Brigade
July 1913	Becomes Corporal, G Company, First Battalion of the British Rifle Brigade
4 August 1914	Rifle Brigade mobilises. Intensive training commences on playing fields of Old Harrow School
22 August 1914	Embarks on SS *Cestrian* and crosses to France
25 August 1914	Arrives at Le Cateau with Brigade to assist Allies in their retreat from Mons
26 August 1914	First action against Germans. Wins Military Medal for bravery in the field. Wounded, and captured by Germans in Ligny Cathedral
September 1914	Arrives as a POW at Döberitz near Berlin after a period of rehabilitation in Braunschweig
June 1917	Jack's father, Charles dies in Melbourne
6 September 1917	Jack escapes from Döberitz
17 September 1917	Crawls from bunker of *Auraor* in Malmö, Sweden a free man. Wins Military Cross
12 October 1917	Enlists in Royal Flying Corps (later RAF)
5 November 1918	Wins his 'wings' and graduates as Second Lieutenant
11 November 1918	Crashes his SE5A while performing celebratory aerobatics on Armistice Day

17 November 1918	Sustains serious injuries in a crash at Turnberry, Scotland
May 1919	Repatriated to Australia after several months rehabilitation
24 July 1924	Wins a dry area Soldier Settlers block at Rankins Springs, New South Wales
8 June 1925	Marries Minnie Cook in Coogee, New South Wales after three-week whirlwind romance. Returns to Rankins Springs
23 December 1927	Minnie leaves with son John, Jack remains on farm
June 1933	Marries Nora Peach in Griffith, New South Wales
21 May 1936	Sherriff is born
October 1938	Walks off farm after long severe drought and establishes a farm produce story in Griffith
22 November 1939	John is born
April 1940	Enlists in AIF. Posted as Acting Warrant Officer to Army Intelligence in Melbourne
August 1940	Leaves with unit for the Middle East
4 February 1941	Mysteriously discharged and returns to Australia
April 1941	Changes name and re-enlists at Paddington, NSW
29 July 1941	Sails with 2/15th Regiment on *Johan van Oldenbarnevelt* for Singapore
8 December 1941	First Japanese landings on Malay peninsula
13 January 1942	Jack's first engagement with Japanese at Gemas
8 February 1942	Battle for Singapore Island begins
15 February 1942	Allied forces surrender. Jack becomes a POW
7 July 1942	Leaves Singapore with 'B' Force on *Yubi Maru* for Borneo
18 July 1942	Arrives in Sandakan
May 1943	Jack's first postcard from Sandakan sent. It arrives in Australia in September 1944 confirming his imprisonment
10 May 1945	Dies in Sandakan and is buried in No. 2 Cemetery just outside the perimeter of the POW camp
15 August 1945	Murozumi beheads last Sandakan POW. Japan surrenders to the Allies
27 August 1945	Last fifteen POWs from Sandakan at Ranau executed and camp abandoned
2 October 1945	Official telegram arrives notifying the family of Jack's death in Sandakan
1947	Jack is reburied in unidentified grave in Labuan War Cemetery

Jack Probert's Family

Reverend Thomas Probert
Jack's great, great grandfather
Born 1729 Herefordshire
BA Lincoln College, Oxford 1750
Ordained rector in 1755
Died 1802

Rebecca **Carwardine**
Four children: Thomas, Anne,
Francis, Rebecca
Died 1824

Thomas **Probert**
Jack's great grandfather
Born 1776
Lived most of his life at Newport
House, home of Probert family
Solicitor in firm of Probert and Wade
Died in 1849

Anne **Carwardine**
Married in 1813, last of Carwardine family of
Colne Priory, first cousin to Thomas. Carwardine
used as Christian name for many descendants.
Five children: Thomas, William, John, Charles,
Anne
Died 1836

William Richard **Probert**
Jack's grandfather
Born 1815 at Newport House
Traveller and adventurer
Captain in East India Company
Arrived in the *Protector* in
Melbourne 1853
Chandler, gold prospector, ship's
surveyor, commission agent
Preacher for Plymouth Brethren in
Melbourne
Died at Bevils in UK in 1903

Elizabeth **Archer**
Born 1833
Married 1850
Lost three still-born sons.
Accompanied William to
Melbourne in 1853
Died, aged 22 in 1855, weeks
after birth of son, Charles in
Williamstown, Victoria
Buried in Brighton Cemetery,
Melbourne

Lucinda **Hunt**
Second wife of William
Probert, married 1863
Six children — William,
Arthur, Norah, Aileen,
Claude, Cyril
Separated in 1871

Charles Moule Verdon **Probert**
Jack's father
Born 1855 in Williamstown, Victoria
Secondary schooling in England
Returned with father to Australia 1872
Lost inheritance. Worked at variety of
jobs; jackarooing and droving in
Queensland, NSW, & NT
Married 1889. Insurance & stock
broker in Collins Street, Melbourne
Member of Melbourne 'establishment'
Died Melbourne in 1917

Maud Mary **Woodward**
Born 1868
Married in 1889 in dual marriage
with sister in Bendigo. Youngest
daughter of family of twelve.
Father Mayor of Bendigo
Marriage consummated three
years after wedding
One son, John
Stormy marriage — divorced in 1901
Remarried in Sydney
Died around 1952

Elsie May **Vanden Hooten**
Born 1888, St Kilda
Second wife of Charles
Married hurriedly, July 190
One son Charles
Remarried
Died 1839
Buried Brighton, Vic.

John (Jack) William [Moule] **Probert**
Born 1893 Melbourne
Windjammer 'boy'
Joined British Rifle Brigade in 1912
German POW 1914-1917; escaped
Won MM and MC
Commissioned Officer in RFC
Soldier settler farmer in NSW
Fought with Second AIF in Singapore
Japanese POW 1942-1945 at Sandakan
Died aged 51
Buried on Labuan Island

Minnie **Cook**
Married in 1925 in Coogee after
three-week whirlwind courtship.
Joined Jack on Soldier Settlers
block near Rankins Springs
Left marriage Christmas, 1927
One son John
Divorced 1933

Nora Gwendoline **Peach**
Second wife of Jack
Born St Albans UK in 1905
Arrived in Australia in 1911
Attended Fort Street
Girls High
Cashier with National Regist
Married in St Albans, Griffit
1933
Two sons, Sherriff and John
Died 1973
Buried in Griffith Cemetery

APPENDIX 4

Notes on Imperial Measures

The action of this story takes place at a time when Australia used Imperial units of measurement. These have been converted to metric measures, except where it would be inappropriate to do so. Brief, approximate conversions are given below.

Metric conversions
1 mile ≈ 1.6 km
1 foot ≈ 30 centimetres
1 acre ≈ 0.40 hectares, 1 hectare = 2.47 acres
1 ton ≈ 1 tonne

Pre-decimal currency – LSD
In Australia's pre-decimal currency, a pound (£) consisted of twenty shillings, and a shilling of 12 pence. This traditional notation for LSD was as follows:

For amounts greater than one pound
£1/10/3 indicated 'one pound, ten shillings, and threepence'
A hyphen was often used to indicate a zero amount, e.g. £2/15/– indicated 'two pounds fifteen shillings (and no pence)'

For amounts less than one pound
12/6 indicated 'twelve shillings and sixpence'

At the time of conversion to decimal currency in 1966, one pound became two dollars, and one shilling became ten cents.

Selected References

ABC Documentary	*Return to Sandakan*, Australian Broadcasting Commission, July 1995.
ABC Documentary	*Borneo: Fiftieth Anniversary of the End of World War 2*, Australian Broadcasting Commission, August, 1995.
Adam-Smith, P.	*Prisoners of War*, Penguin, Ringwood, 1997.
Anon.	*The Link: A Souvenir Book Published by British POWs Interned at Döberitz Germany 1914–18*, Schoneberg, Berlin, 1918.
Arneil, S.	*One Man's War*, Macmillan, Sydney, 1980.
Bean, C.E.W	*The Australian Flying Corps in The Official History of Australians in the War 1914–1918, Volume 8*, Australian War Memorial, 1938.
Bowden, T.	Interview with R. Braithwaite from unedited tape transcripts *Australia Under Nippon*, Australian Broadcasting Commission, 1983
Burgess, C.	'In the Footsteps of the Dead', in *Freedom and Death: Australia's Greatest Escape Stories from Two World Wars*, Allen and Unwin, 1994.
Brown, M.	*The First World War.*
Bryant, A.	*Jackets of Green: A Study of the History, Philosophy and Character of the Rifle Brigade*, Collins, London, 1972.
British Rifle Brigade	*First Battalion: Field Diary 24 August–29 September, 1914*, Green Jackets Museum, Winchester.
Dennett, C.P.	*Prisoners of the Great War: Authoritative Statements of Conditions in the Prison Camps of Germany*, Houghton Mifflin, 1919.
Cimino, H.	*Behind the Prison Bars in Germany*, Newnes, 1915.
Eastwood, J.	*Melbourne: The Growth of a Metropolis: Commentary and Documents*, Nelson, 1983.

Enser, A.G.S.	*A Subject Bibliography of the First World War: Books in English*, Second Edition, Gower, 1993.
Gilliland, H.G.	*My German Prisons*, Hodder and Stoughton, 1918.
Harvey, B.	*The Rifle Brigade*, Cooper, London, 1975.
Harvey, F.W.	*Comrades in Captivity: A Record of Life in Seven German Prison Camps*, Sidgwick and Jackson, London, 1920.
Hennebois, C.	*In German Hands*, Heinemann, London, 1916.
Hoffman, C.	*In the Prison Camps of Germany: A Narrative of Y Service Among the Prisoners of War*, Association Press: New York, 1920.
Holley, K.	*Rankins Springs Golden Jubilee 1926–1976 Souvenir Booklet*, 1976.
Kiddle, J.B.	*War Services of Old Melburnians, 1914–1918*, Arbuckle, Waddle & Fawkner, Melbourne, 1922.
Mahony, H.C.	*Interned in Germany*, Sampson Low Marston, London, 1918.
Masters, J.	*Fourteen Eighteen: Mons and Le Cateau.*
Moynihan, M.	*Black Bread and Barbed Wire*, Cooper, London, 1978.
Murray, R.	*The Confident Years: Australia in the Twenties*, Allen Lane, 1978.
NSW Government	*Land for Soldiers*, Government Printer, February 1918.
Parsons, A. and Guiton, J.	*Conapaira Links 1858–1998*, Historical Society, Rankins Springs, 1999.
Pye, E.	*Prisoner of War*, Revell, New York, 1938.
Roberts, S.	*History of Australian Land Settlement 1788–1920*, Macmillan, Melbourne, 1924.
Silver, L.	*Sandakan: A Conspiracy of Silence*, Second Edition, Milner, Canberra, 2000.
Verner, W.	*History and Campaigns of the Rifle Brigade 1914–1919*, Bale and Sons, London, 1920.
Wall, D.	*The Last March: Sandakan under Nippon*, Wall, Mona Vale, 1988.

Westlake, R.	*The Rifle Brigade (The Prince Consort's Own) in British Battalions in France and Belgium 1914*, Cooper, London, 1997.
Whitlock, G.	'Escape from German Prison Camp', *Sydney Morning Herald*, 3 December 1938.
Whitelocke, C.	*Gunners in the Jungle*, 2/15th Field Regiment Association, 1983.
Wilmot, R.W.E. (ed.)	*A History of the Church of England Grammar School, Melbourne*. Arbuckle, Waddle & Fawkner, Melbourne, 1914.
Yong, Y.S., Bose, R., Pang, A.	*Fortress Singapore: The Battlefield Guide*, Times Books International, Singapore, 1992.

Index

ALSO BY WAKEFIELD PRESS

Mudeye

An Australian boyhood and beyond

Bary Dowling

Here is a snapshot of Australia as it once was, of old gold town Ballarat during the second world war occupation by American troops. There are shades of *All Creatures Great and Small* as a vet and his son travel the country together, but this childhood story grows and matures into a haunting spiritual journey. Bary Dowling is a reviewer, nature writer and travel writer who has been a farmer and gardener for most of his working life.

1 86254 345 3 $19.95

ALSO BY WAKEFIELD PRESS

Fallout

Hedley Marston and the British bomb tests in Australia

Roger Cross

In the 1950s the Australian government agreed to let the British government test atomic bombs in South Australia's northern deserts. The Australian public was assured there was no risk from radioactive fallout, but one man wasn't satisfied. Hedley Marston was a CSIRO biochemist whose experiments proved the government's Safety Committee were telling lies. *Fallout* is the story of a government desperate for prestige and one man willing to risk everything to expose the danger of radioactive fallout.

1 86254 523 5 $24.95

On My Brothers' Shoulders

Ty Andre with Allen McMahon

A story of remarkable achievement. – Jack Thompson

One evening in 1952, a young woman walked down to the Mekong River carrying her baby boy in a home-made basket. She lit a candle and stood it in the basket, then set her baby adrift on the stream. Miraculously, the child was rescued by a fisherman and taken to a Catholic mission on the island of Cu Lao Gieng. The little boy was named 'Ty', meaning 'billion', because his chances of surviving were a billion to one. This is the story of that one-in-a-billion chance.

1 86254 378 X $19.95

ALSO BY WAKEFIELD PRESS

Dune is a Four-letter Word

Desert crossings and dusty memories

Griselda Sprigg with Rod Maclean

Foreword by Dick Smith

It was 1962. 'Dune is a four-letter word,' said Griselda Sprigg on the first day of her family's attempt to make the first motorised crossing of the forbidding Simpson desert. 'And so is bloody spinifex.'

The Spriggs were never mere bush-bashers. Their adventures in the Australian outback had science and the pursuit of knowledge as a central core. Griselda's story is like the woman herself. It is earthy and humorous and it displays Griselda's deep love for her family and for Australia's wondrous arid zones. – Dick Smith

HB 1 86254 516 2 $45.00
PB 1 86254 540 5 $27.50

Wakefield Press has been publishing good Australian books
for over fifty years. For a catalogue of current and
forthcoming titles, or to add your name to our mailing list,
send your name and address to
Wakefield Press, Box 2266, Kent Town, South Australia 5071.

TELEPHONE (08) 8362 8800 FAX (08) 8362 7592
WEB www.wakefieldpress.com.au

Government
of South Australia   A R T **S** A

Wakefield Press thanks Arts South Australia
for its continued support.